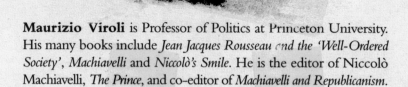

Maurizio Viroli is Professor of Politics at Princeton University. His many books include *Jean Jacques Rousseau and the 'Well-Ordered Society'*, *Machiavelli* and *Niccolò's Smile*. He is the editor of Niccolò Machiavelli, *The Prince*, and co-editor of *Machiavelli and Republicanism*.

HOW TO READ

MACHIAVELLI

MAURIZIO VIROLI

GRANTA

Granta Publications, 12 Addison Avenue, London W11 4QR

First published in Great Britain by Granta Books, 2008

Copyright © Maurizio Viroli, 2008

A CIP catalogue record for this book is
available from the British Library.

1 3 5 7 9 10 8 6 4 2

ISBN 978 1 86207 991 5

Typeset by M Rules

Printed and bound in Great Britain
by CPI Bookmarque, Croydon

CONTENTS

SERIES EDITOR'S FOREWORD

How am I to read *How to Read*?

This series is based on a very simple, but novel idea. Most beginners' guides to great thinkers and writers offer either potted biographies or condensed summaries of their major works, or perhaps even both. *How to Read*, by contrast, brings the reader face to face with the writing itself in the company of an expert guide. Its starting point is that in order to get close to what a writer is all about, you have to get close to the words they actually use and be shown how to read those words.

Every book in the series is in a way a masterclass in reading. Each author has selected ten or so short extracts from a writer's work and looks at them in detail as a way of revealing their central ideas and thereby opening doors onto a whole world of thought. Sometimes these extracts are arranged chronologically to give a sense of a thinker's development over time, sometimes not. The books are not merely compilations of a thinker's most famous passages, their 'greatest hits', but rather they offer a series of clues or keys that will enable readers to go on and make discoveries of their own. In addition to the texts and readings, each book provides a short biographical chronology and suggestions for further reading, Internet resources, and so on. The books in the *How to Read* series don't claim to tell you all you need to know about Freud, Nietzsche and Darwin, or indeed Shakespeare and the Marquis de Sade, but they do offer the best starting point for further exploration.

Unlike the available second-hand versions of the minds that have shaped our intellectual, cultural, religious, political and scientific landscape, *How to Read* offers a refreshing set of first-hand encounters with those minds. Our hope is that these books will, by turn, instruct, intrigue, embolden, encourage and delight.

Simon Critchley
New School for Social Research, New York

NOTES ON THE TEXT

When referencing English translations I have used abbreviations. References are to books and chapters, except for letters and *The Chief Works*, for which I use page numbers. I have revised the translations where necessary.

P: *The Prince*, ed. and trans. Peter Bondanella with an Introduction by Maurizio Viroli (Oxford University Press, 2005).

D: *Discourses on Livy*, trans. Harvey C. Mansfield and Nathan Tarcov (University of Chicago Press, 1998).

AW: *The Art of War*, Christopher Lynch (ed.) (University of Chicago Press, 2003).

FH: *Florentine Histories*, ed. and trans. Laura F. Banfield and Harvey C. Mansfield Jr. (Princeton University Press, 1990).

OW: *Machiavelli: The Chief Works and Others*, ed. and trans. Allan Gilbert (Durham, NC, Duke University Press, 1965), 3 vols.

L: *Machiavelli and his Friends: Their Personal Correspondence*, James B. Atkinson and David Sices (eds) (Dekalb, Northern Illinois University Press, 1996).

For the Italian text I have used Niccolò Machiavelli, *Opere*, Corrado Vivanti (ed.) (Turin, Einaudi, 1997–2005), 3 vols.

INTRODUCTION

To understand the meaning of Machiavelli's writings one must put aside, or at least question, a number of widespread beliefs about his work that are still held by scholars and the general public. Most of these beliefs reflect conceptions that emerged much later in the history of political ideas. The first step to an intelligent reading of Machiavelli's political ideas is to consider his political and intellectual context.

He was born (3 May 1469) in Florence at a time when the powerful Medici family dominated the political life of the city. He witnessed in 1494 the French King Charles VIII's invasion, which marked the first step toward the end of Italy's independence and the birth of a new republican government under the moral and political inspiration of a Dominican friar, Girolamo Savonarola, who was then tried and executed under the charge of heresy in 1498. Under the republican government Machiavelli served as a high-rank executive in charge of supervising foreign affairs and matters pertaining to the Florentine dominions. In 1512, however, the Republic fell down under the combined attack of Spanish and papal troops, opening the way to the full restoration of a new Medicean regime. Machiavelli not only lost his post but was later imprisoned and tortured under the charge of conspiracy against the new governors of Florence. From that fatal year until his death (1527), he mainly devoted himself to the composition of his great political and historical essays: *The Prince* (1513), the *Discourses on Livy* (1513–19), *The Art of War* (1521) and the *Florentine Histories*, as well as his comedies and poetical works, in particular *Mandragola* (1518) and *The [Golden] Ass*. Of all his political and historical works only *The Art of War* was published during his lifetime (1521); *The Prince* appeared in 1532, *The Discourses* in 1531. After 1512 he was never able to obtain important political positions and in the last years of his life he struggled in vain to prevent Italy from falling under foreign domination. While almost all scholars have considered him purely as a political theorist, he also offers a powerful moral philosophy based upon the belief that the misery of the human condition can be escaped by devotion to great ideals. He was severe on human malignity but looked on human weakness with a benevolent and ironic smile. His conception of life reflected in this sense Italian Renaissance moral philosophy.

In spite of his impeccable honesty and intense devotion to the common good of his Republic and of Italy, it is commonplace to consider him the teacher and advocate of the perfidious principle that in politics 'the end justifies the means'; that political action cannot be judged on the moral principles of justice and integrity that we employ to evaluate ordinary individuals' actions, but only from the standpoint of success. Yet the plain truth is that Niccolò Machiavelli never wrote this sentence, nor proffered that the conquest or preservation of political power justifies the use of cruelty, deceit, and unfaithfulness. He distinguishes between a tyranny and a principality or a republic, and he asserts that tyrants are the most despicable human beings: 'Among all men praised, the most praised are those who have been heads and orderers of religions. Next, then, are those who have founded either republics or kingdoms [. . .] On the contrary, men are infamous and detestable who are destroyers of religion, squanderers of kingdoms and republics, and enemies of the virtues, of letters and of every other art that brings utility and honour to the human race, as are the impious, the violent, the ignorant, the worthless, the idle, the cowardly. And no one will ever be so crazy or so wise, so wicked or so good, who will not praise what is to be praised and blame what is to be blamed, when the choice between the two qualities of men is placed before him.'

Even a glorious political end, like the foundation of a good kingdom or a good republic, can at best excuse, not justify, the use of immoral means. The accomplishment of founding new states is most glorious of all if not only immoral means are avoided, but violence altogether: 'no man is so much exalted by any act of his as are those men who have with laws and with institutions reformed republics and kingdoms; these are, after those who have been gods, the first to be praised' (*OW*, i.115). Even when the deed is glorious, crimes perpetrated to attain it cannot be washed away, whereas a good political goal attained by right means is worthy of the highest praise.

Machiavelli, then, did not advise princes and leaders of republics to 'do all it takes to seize and preserve power'. Rather, he urged political leaders to pursue the true glory that comes from founding good political orders with good means. By killing one's fellow citizens, betraying allies, being without faith, without pity, without religion, 'one can acquire power but not glory' (*P*, VIII). Machiavelli's wording is of crucial importance. Glory is for him the goal that princes and great leaders ought to pursue. A prince should perpetrate an action that gives power without glory only as a last resort. Thus Machiavelli notes that a man like Agathocles, tyrant of Syracuse – who was unique in overcoming adversities and equal to any most excellent commander – had a 'vicious cruelty and inhumanity', which does 'not permit us to honour him among the most excellent of men' (*P*, VIII). Political leaders only go down the path of evil when no other means to a good political deed are available, and return to the right path as soon as possible. His greatest hero was Moses, who 'was forced to kill infinite men who, moved by nothing other than envy were opposed to his plan' (*D*, III.30). Nonetheless, God was and remained his friend. Machiavelli's political teaching is that God himself is prepared to pardon an act of cruelty, avarice or unfaithfulness when necessary for a good political end. This conception of political ethics, which Machiavelli believes a good man ought to counsel, is for many readers surely much more offensive than the old platitude 'the end justifies the means', but it is a different idea.

Another misleading commonplace views Machiavelli's works as objective studies of political life and Machiavelli as one of the forerunners of the contemporary science of politics. 'What Galileo gave in his *Dialogues*, and what Machiavelli gave in his *Prince*,' wrote Ernst Cassirer, 'were really "new sciences". Just as Galileo Dynamics became the foundation of our modern science of nature, so Machiavelli paved a new way to political science.'[1] Cassirer's and others' analysis overlooks Machiavelli's intentions: he composed all his political and historical works, not only to describe and explain facts, as scientists do, but above all to persuade his readers to act, as orators do. If we continue to read *The Prince* and his other works as scientific texts, we simply fail to understand what kind of works we are reading, and we miss the author's intent.

His goal was to impel readers to act by touching their minds and passions, and to achieve this he wrote the manuscript following the rules of classical rhetoric, as all the humanists of his time did. Born and educated in a city that considered eloquence the highest ornament of free political life and a necessary component of the education of a good citizen, Machiavelli had fully absorbed this style of thinking and writing. Moreover, his work as Secretary of the Second Chancery of the Republic of Florence, under the supervision of the renowned scholar Marcello Virgilio Adriani, required the practice of political rhetoric, particularly when writing letters to the leading committees of the Republic on matters of domestic and foreign policy and in the composition of orations for the highest magistrates of the Republic. Both his letters and orations had to please men educated to appreciate good style and persuasive prose, and they reveal a secure mastery of rhetoric.

The Prince, which many readers consider a handbook of political science, is a long oration. Like all good Renaissance orations it begins with an appropriate preface (*exordium*). The 'Dedicatory letter to His Magnificence Lorenzo de' Medici' renders the reader well disposed and attentive. In Machiavelli's case, the task was particularly delicate because he was the former Secretary of the Republic and a man of low social status who dared to write on state matters, an uncommon practice in his times. The preface needed to remove the ill-disposition of the Medici. Machiavelli gains the reader's benevolence by promoting his good qualities, the services he has rendered, his competence on matters of state, describing the hardships he has endured and the ill-fortune that malignantly strikes him. He claims that to be a man of lower social status actually puts him in the best position to treat matters of state: 'I hope it will not be considered presumptuous for a man of very low and humble condition to dare to discuss princely government, and to lay down rules about it. For those who draw maps place themselves on low ground, in order to understand the character of the plain. Likewise, one needs to be a ruler to properly understand the character of the people, and to be a man of the people to properly understand the character of rulers.'

The clearest evidence that *The Prince* is an oration is the 'Exhortation to liberate Italy from the barbarians' that closes the work. Without the 'Exhortation', Machiavelli's essay would have lacked the necessary device to arouse the readers' emotions and move them to act. He constructs the 'Exhortation' to instil indignation and compassion, hardly the preoccupation of a scientist. He arouses indignation by stressing the cruelties and insolences that the barbarians have inflicted upon Italy, and excites compassion by pointing to Italy's weakness and helplessness: 'more enslaved than the Hebrews, more servile than the Persians, more scattered than the Athenians: without a leader, without order, beaten, despoiled, ripped apart, overrun, and having suffered every sort of ruin' (*P*, XXVI). Far from being inconsistent with the rest of the work, as some commentators have suggested, the 'Exhortation' is the perfect ending.

In all his works Machiavelli reports ancient and modern historical examples to make his arguments vivid, lucid and
persuasive; to rouse the desire to imitate great political and military leaders: 'nobody should be surprised if, in discussing
completely new principalities, both as regards the rulers and
the type of government, I shall cite very great examples' because
a prudent man must always follow the footsteps of great men,
and even if 'he does not succeed in matching their ability, at
least he will get within a sniffing distance of it' (*P*, VI). For the
same reason he uses similes, images and metaphors. When he
explains that a prince must be capable of using both fraud and
force, he demonstrates this through the images of the lion
and the fox. When he proclaims that a prince should never
rely upon auxiliary armies, he finds in the Old Testament a
'figure' particularly 'apt for this purpose': 'When David offered
to Saul to go and fight Goliath, the Philistine challenger, Saul,
to give him spirit, armed him with his own arms – which
David, as soon as he had them on, refused, saying that with
them he could not give a good account of himself, and so he
would rather meet the enemy with his sling and his knife'
(*P*, XIII).

To present Machiavelli as an orator rather than a political
scientist may damage his reputation among readers and scholars
who believe that political life should be investigated through
methods similar to those of the other social sciences or even
through mathematical tools. In my opinion, the study of politics
based upon historical knowledge is much more effective
than the scientific approach that began to conquer intellectual
predominance in the eighteenth century. To stress that Machiavelli
was an orator elevates his status over contemporary scholars, and,
most importantly, restores the historical truth.

Yet another popular image is Machiavelli as the prototype of
political machismo, political action taken by anxious and defen-
sive men proving their manliness by asserting autonomy and
rationality against 'feminine' dependence and irrationality. Yet,

even if he lived in an unequal society, when Machiavelli talks of real women he uses a language of equality. He calls Riccia, a courtesan who was for years his lover, his woman-friend ('amica'). He portrays women as equal, and at times he is their subordinate. Riccia speaks to him like a male friend. When she is tired of the penniless Niccolò, she calls him 'house-nuisance', like Machiavelli's old friend Donato del Corno calls him 'shop-nuisance' (L, 278). Machiavelli also describes equality and friendship with women in *The [Golden] Ass* (VI, 25–7), a poem that contains several autobiographical allusions. After some time, says the hero of the story, 'she [Circe's damsel] and I talked together of many things, as one friend speaks to another'. 'Another', in the Italian, is rendered in the masculine ('l'altro'); they conversed in the way a man chats with a man-friend, as equals.

Machiavelli's writings and his life amply illustrate that he was prepared to trade the 'masculine' value of autonomy with the 'feminine' value of dependence and was very keen to yield to the passions. 'I do not know,' Francesco Vettori wrote to him on 16 January 1515, 'what delights more than to fuck or to think of fucking. Men can philosophize as they please, but this is the pure truth' (L, 311). Machiavelli responds with a sonnet on the power of love and says that even if he knew the way to free himself of the chains of love, he would not use it, because 'so much now sweet, now light, now heavy do I find those chains, and they make a mixture of such a sort that I judge I cannot live contented without that kind of life' (L, 312). He knows that love will bring him much pain, but the perception of woman's beauty is too overwhelming and seductive: 'I feel in it such sweetness, both through what that face so wonderful and soft brings me, and also through having laid aside the memory of all my troubles, that for anything in the world, being able to free myself, I would not wish it' (L, 293). If the assertion of autonomy is the distinctive feature of machismo, Niccolò does not deserve the title.

Over the centuries Machiavelli has been regarded as a counsellor of tyrants, as a fervent republican, or as a man ready to
serve any master to gain power. Yet in 1521, when the former
Gonfalonier of the Republic of Florence and his political patron,
Pier Soderini, offered Machiavelli a highly rewarded post as secretary of the condottiere Prospero Colonna, he refused even
though he was for the most part unemployed – at the time his
only job was a commission by Cardinal Giulio de' Medici to
write the history of Florence for a small sum. Earlier on he had
also turned down an offer to become the chancellor of the
Republic of Ragusa. Machiavelli was not prepared to serve just
any powerful man.

Rather than seeking public office, Machiavelli was eager to see
his competence on the art of the state, and his uprightness, properly recognized. In the famous letter to Francesco Vettori of 10
December 1513, he revealed his great desire that the Medici
employ him even with a paltry task. He knew well 'the art of the
state' ['arte dello stato'], and had always served the Republic with
impeccable honesty. He was asking the Medici to read his 'little'
work and to consider what he had done for Florence: 'for if I
should not then win them over to me, I should complain myself;
and through this thing [the manuscript of *The Prince*], if it were
read, one would see that I have neither slept through nor played
away the fifteen years I have been at the study of the art of the
state. And anyone should be glad to have the service of one who
is full of experience at the expense of another. And one should
not doubt my faith, because having always observed faith, I
ought not now to be learning to break it. Whoever has been
faithful and good for forty-three years, as I have, ought not to be
able to change his nature, and of my faith and goodness my
poverty is witness.' These are not the words of a courtesan beg-
ging to serve any regime, but of a citizen willing to serve his
country, and of a man eager to accomplish great deeds.

When he was no longer a high-rank counsellor because of the
persistent hostility of the Medici family, Machiavelli accepted

very humble assignments: in 1521 he was sent to Carpi, near Modena, as Orator of Florence to the General Assembly of the Franciscan Order, to transact a minor business for the Medici. When he arrived in Carpi, he received a request from the Officer of the Florentine Art of the Wool to carry out an even more inglorious mission – to find a Lenten preacher. Even if the mission was an insult to his talents and his reputation, he served his country to the best of his abilities: 'And because I never failed that city by not benefiting her when I could – if not with deeds, with words, if not with words, with gestures – I do not intend to fail her this time either.' He was practising what he preached. In the *Discourses* he had written that 'Citizens who have had great honours should not disdain lesser ones' (*D*, I.36).

Machiavelli's most valuable service was accomplished with his writings on republican theory of political liberty. He composed the *Discourses on Livy* to resurrect Roman republican political wisdom and developed upon it a body of reflections on the form of government and the civic ethos best suited to ensure liberty and civic greatness. He also wrote *The Art of War* to retrieve and put into practice Roman military institutions on the basis of the idea that good political institutions need good armies (*AW*, Preface, 4–5). In his last great work, the *Florentine Histories*, he urges his fellow Florentines to avoid the tragic mistakes of their ancestors that caused the loss of liberty and the decay of the city, but to follow instead the true principles of republican politics that would lead to a free and civil way of life.

As later political theorists openly admitted, Machiavelli's insights marked a deep watershed within republican tradition. This tradition had its intellectual roots in ancient Greek and Roman political thinking and had developed over the centuries a large body of reflections on political liberty and on its institutional and moral foundations. But it is only with Machiavelli that republican political ideas are confronted with the full range of problems of modern society in general and modern Italy in particular. For this reason, and also because of the elegance of his style of writing, all republican thinkers of modern times took inspiration and learned from his works, even when they were critical of his ideas.

The effects of Machiavelli's writings throughout history are not conclusive evidence of his political convictions. However, I strongly believe that he was a convinced republican and a strenuous opponent of tyranny. He never became a partisan of the Medici regime, as two very distinguished scholars have recently claimed. The Medici regime (1512–27) was in effect a principality, where the most prominent members of the family controlled the political life of the city. For this reason Machiavelli never wrote to praise their regime and the Medici never recognized him as one of their many friends. Machiavelli explicitly contended that republican governments are better than monarchies: 'as to prudence and stability, I say that a people is more prudent, more stable, and of better judgement than a prince. If it [the people] errs in mighty things or those that appear useful, as is said above, often a prince errs too in his passions, which are many more than those of peoples. It is also seen in its choices of magistrates to make a better choice by far than a prince; nor will a people ever be persuaded that it is good to put up for dignities an infamous man of corrupt customs – of which a prince is persuaded easily and by a thousand ways.' Beyond this, he explains, 'one sees that cities in which peoples are princes make exceeding increases in every brief time, and much greater than those that have always been made under a prince, as did Rome after the expulsion of the kings and Athens after it was freed from Pisistratus. That cannot arise from anything other than that governments of peoples are better than those of prince' (D, I.58).

Equally compelling evidence of Machiavelli's republicanism is his proposal for a constitutional reform in Florence, composed in 1521 upon Cardinal Giulio de' Medici's insistence. In this text Machiavelli openly counsels the powerful cardinal to restore the republican government. Because of its tradition of equality, he explains, Florence cannot endure a principate, and to impose one would be a cruel and blameworthy action. In that city one cannot have a stable republic without satisfying the people, and the only way to satisfy the people is to 'reopen the hall', that is to restore the Republic. It is hard to imagine a more explicitly republican position, a position all the more important because Machiavelli sustains it in a text addressed to a Medici cardinal who was the *de facto* ruler of Florence.

Machiavelli composed not only important political and historical works, but also *Mandragola*, one of the best pieces of Italian theatre. He wrote it in around 1518, probably one of the saddest years of his life. By that time he had been unemployed for six years, and he had lost all hope of obtaining a new post in Florence or Rome. Almost all his old friends had deserted him, and he and his family were surviving on the meagre resources of their countryside properties. He even contemplated abandoning Florence and his family to teach children to read and write. Instead he remained in his city and composed a play that would make an audience laugh. If this story does not suit a man who wants to appear wise and grave, he writes, 'make this excuse for him, that he is striving with these trifling thoughts to make his wretched life more pleasant for otherwise he doesn't know where to turn his face, since he has been cut off from showing other powers with other deeds, there being no pay for his labours'. No captains, no lawgivers, no princes: the heroes of his play are 'a doleful lover, a judge by no means shrewd, a wicked friar, a parasite beloved by Malice'. The story is not designed to instil the desire to imitate grand example of virtue, but simply to provoke laughter: 'if you do not laugh,' he writes, I am ready 'to pay for your wine' (*OW*, II.776–7).

Machiavelli was both able to write grave works on serious political issues and to appreciate lightness, irony, and self-irony. He lived by this philosophy and even theorized it: 'anybody who saw our letters, honoured friend, and saw their diversity,' he wrote to Vettori, 'would wonder greatly, because he would suppose now that we were grave men, wholly concerned with important matters, and that into our breasts no thought could fall that did not have in itself honour and greatness. But then, turning the page, he would judge that we, the very same persons, were light-minded, inconstant, lascivious, concerned with empty things. And this way of proceeding, if to some it may appear censurable, to me it seems praiseworthy, because we are imitating Nature who is variable; and he who imitates her cannot be rebuked' (*L*, 961–2). Very few political theorists have been able to combine, as Machiavelli did, different orders of thought: the serious and the trivial, the ordinary and the grand, the contingent and the infinite. It is precisely his particular wisdom and his deep humanness that makes his works worth reading today.

1

THE LOVE OF POLITICS AND OTHER LOVES

When evening has come, I return to my house and go into my study. At the door I take off my clothes of the day, covered with mud and mire, and I put on my regal and courtly garments; and decently reclothed, I enter the ancient courts of ancient men, where, received by them lovingly, I feed on the food that alone is mine and that I was born for. There I am not ashamed to speak with them and to ask them the reasons for their actions; and they in their humanity reply to me. And for the space of four hours I feel no boredom; I forget every pain, I do not fear poverty, death does not frighten me. I deliver myself entirely to them. And because Dante says that to have understood without retaining does not make knowledge, I have noted what capital I have made from their conversation and have composed a little work *De Principatibus* [*The Prince*, even if the correct translation would be On Principalities], where I delve as deeply as I can into reflections on this subject, debating what a principality is, of what kind they are, how they are acquired, how they are maintained, why they are lost. And if you have ever been pleased by any of my whimsies, this one should not displease you; and to a prince, and especially to a new prince, it should be welcome. So I am addressing it to his Magnificence, Giuliano. Filippo Casavecchia has seen it; he can give you an account in part both of the thing in itself and on the discussion I had with him, although I am all

the time fattening and polishing it. [. . .] The necessity that
chases me makes me give it, because I am becoming worn out,
and I cannot remain as I am for a long time without becoming
despised because of poverty, besides the desire I have that these
Medici lords begin to make use of me even if they should begin
by making me roll a stone. For if I should not then win them over
to me, I should complain of myself; and through this thing, if it
were read, one would see that I have neither slept through nor
played away the fifteen years I have been at the study of the art
of the state. And anyone should be glad to have the service of one
who is full of experience at the expense of another.

From the letter to Vettori of 10 December 1513

In this letter to Francesco Vettori, Ambassador of the Republic
of Florence at the papal court in Rome, Machiavelli reveals his
inner world, and we perceive, at least in part, what kind of
person was the author of *The Prince* and the *Discourses on Livy.*
His two greatest passions were the love of politics and the love
of women. A profound sense of grief had led him to open his
soul to a friend. One year before, he had lost his position as
Secretary of the Second Chancery of the Republic of Florence.
The new regime imposed by the powerful Medici family, which
had transformed the Republic into a veiled principality, had
prohibited him from the Palazzo Vecchio, the core of Florence's
political life. He was living in the countryside, with his family,
distant from power, from great deeds, from the intensity of civil
life, and even from friends, except for the very few who
remained close to him after his political defeat. In this period of
his life he composed his most important political work, *The
Prince.* Machiavelli was not an academic who wrote books in
order to display his knowledge of a subject, nor was he a cold
writer of political advice. On the contrary, he brought his passions and soul to his books. If we want to understand his works
through the dense clouds of time and prejudice, we must begin
with the man.

Machiavelli has a reputation as a demonic figure, a 'teacher of evil', who composed his works under Satan's direct inspiration. Yet he was a citizen of impeccable honesty and uprightness. Having dismissed him from office, the new regime investigated him to verify if he was guilty of illegalities and above all whether he had taken the Republic's money for himself. Since he was in charge, among other duties, of paying soldiers, large sums of money passed many times through his hands. But not even a jury appointed by a hostile political regime was able to prove any misconduct. As Machiavelli proudly remarked more than once, 'my poverty is the evidence of my honesty'. And when he served the Republic of Florence, before 1512, he did it with the utmost unrelenting and accurate devotion, sparing himself no danger, no hardship or fatigue, despite the ingratitude, suspicion and even open hostility, often motivated by envy, of the Florentine aristocracy. Machiavelli's only revenge against men's wickedness was to compose a short poem on ingratitude, in 1508. Public service was always for him a matter of personal honour, a duty of his own conscience, and as such to be fulfilled.

In his private life, Machiavelli felt a sincere and lasting affection for his wife Marietta Corsini. She was passionately in love with him, and fiercely lamented his frequent and long absences from home when the governors of Florence sent him on diplomatic missions. The tone of her complaints and remonstrations reveal that she was not at all intimidated by her husband and openly displayed her feelings. Niccolò responded with words of gentle reprobation and made fun of her protests. When he returned home it was a joy for everyone. He called his family 'my brigade', the same word that he used for his friends in Florence. For his family he was a source of reassurance. 'Since you have promised that you will be with us,' wrote his son Guido in 1527, 'we no longer worry' about the German army coming from the Alps, and 'mona Marietta no longer thinks about it' (L, 417). He tried, as much as he could, to be close to all of them, and was hoping for a better future for his sons and daughters, if they deserved it: 'If God grants life to you and me, I believe I can make you a man of standing, if you wish to play your part as you should.' And the part that his son Guido should play was to 'do well and learn', because what gives true honour, he reminds his son, is virtue (*L*, 413). Virtue enriched by compassion, as demonstrated in a letter he wrote to Guido about a crazy mule, saying, 'I want you to treat him quite differently from other crazy creatures, because the other crazy ones are tied up, and I want you to untie him. Give him to Vangelo and tell him to lead him onto Monte Pugliano and take off his bridle and halter and let him go where he will get his living and rid himself of his madness. The territory is large; the animal is small; he can do no harm' (*L*, 413). A little animal who has become crazy should be left free: a fine lesson on liberty and compassion for unfortunate and defenceless creatures, a moral philosophy of the highest kind.

In his youth Machiavelli was exposed to Friar Girolamo Savonarola's preaching. He probably learnt from him, and from Florentine political tradition, his admiration for republican values: that rulers must devote all their energies to serve the common good, that political liberty is the highest value, and that citizens must display an outstanding degree of civic virtue, if they want to live in freedom and resist the enemies of liberty. Like Savonarola, he considered excessively wealthy men a serious threat to republican liberty because they were able, with their money, to bestow favours and protection in exchange for obedience and loyalty, corrupting the moral and political life of the Republic. He wanted to see his fellow Florentines become more virtuous citizens, but he never entertained the thought, as Savonarola did, of transforming them into saints dedicated to the practice of Christian values. Machiavelli loved pleasures, and works of intellectual and artistic beauty. Dante, Petrarch, Boccaccio and the Latin love poets were his favourite writers. One of Boccaccio's maxims inspired his life – that it is better to do and repent than not to do and repent.

Niccolò transformed all his relationships into relationships of friendship. He behaved like a friend to his subordinates in the Palazzo Vecchio. Like his wife and his children, they complained when he was away from Florence because they missed, in addition to his protection, his irresistible humour and special talent in telling and inventing stories. Except for his political enemies, and he had many within the Florentine oligarchy, everyone loved his company, especially women. He had a fair number of love affairs, some of which were nothing more than erotic encounters; others which were inspired by intense fascination; others which were sustained by profound companionship. His long affair with the courtesan Lucrezia, whom he called 'la Riccia', was intensely erotic, and yet he found in her support and comprehension during the darkest years of his life, when he was powerless and penniless.

Forced to abandon the practice of politics, Machiavelli wrote about it at length. He considered it the arena where the highest moral and intellectual qualities could be displayed. In the extract that opens this chapter, he describes how he envelops himself in the authors that he is reading, just like a lover envelops himself in the person he or she loves. When he thinks of politics, he enters another, higher, and nobler world. He is resuscitated by the great historians and political leaders of antiquity; their nourishment gives true life to his soul, redeems and liberates him from boredom, from the fear of poverty, and the fear of death. When he reflects upon the political wisdom of the ancients Machiavelli engages in a twofold effort of redemption: he redeems their wisdom from oblivion, and redeems himself from the abject condition into which the malignity of men and fortune has forced him. His political writing and his political thinking are sustained and inspired by a deep and special religiosity.

In this spirit he composed his major political works: he wished to take his place among the great men of antiquity and to be recognized as a true expert in the art of the state by the great men of the centuries to come. Corrupt and mediocre politicians – as almost all politicians of his times were – would not understand, let alone appreciate, his works. Instead, he composed *The Prince* to teach and inspire a future redeemer of Italy, and the *Discourses on Livy* to teach and educate future founders and leaders of free republics.

2

A REALIST WITH IMAGINATION

Now, it remains to be considered what should be the methods and principles of a prince in dealing with his subjects and allies. Because I know that many have written about this, I am afraid that by writing about it again I shall be considered presumptuous, especially since in discussing this material I depart from the orders of others. But since my intention is to write something useful for anyone who understands it, it seemed more suitable for me to search after the effectual truth of the matter rather than its imagined one. Many writers have imagined republics and principalities that have never been seen nor known to exist in reality. For there is such a distance between how one lives and how one ought to live that anyone who abandons what is done for what ought to be done learns his downfall rather than his preservation. A man who wishes to profess goodness at all times will come to ruin among so many who are not good. Therefore, it is necessary for a prince who wishes to maintain himself to learn how not to be good, and to use this knowledge or not to use it according to necessity.

Leaving aside, therefore, the imagined things concerning a prince, and taking into account those that are true, let me say that all men, when they are spoken of, and especially princes, since they are placed on a higher level, are judged by some of those qualities that bring them either blame or praise. And this is why one is considered generous, another miserly – to use a Tuscan word, since 'avaricious' in our language is still used to mean one who wishes to acquire by means of theft; we call 'miserly' one who excessively avoids using what he has. One is considered a giver, the other rapacious; one cruel, the other merciful; one a breaker of faith, the other faithful; one effeminate and cowardly, the other fierce and courageous; one humane, the other proud; one lascivious, the other chaste; one trustworthy, the other shrewd; one hard, the other easy-going; one serious, the other frivolous; one religious, the other unbelieving; and the like. And I know that everyone will admit it would be a very praiseworthy thing to find in a prince those qualities mentioned above that are held to be good. But since it is neither possible to have them nor to observe them all completely, because the human condition does not permit it, a prince must be prudent enough to know how to escape the infamy of those vices that would take the state away from him, and be on guard against those vices that will not take it from him, whenever possible. But if he cannot, he need not concern himself unduly if he ignores these less serious vices. Moreover, he need not worry about incurring the infamy of those vices without which it would be difficult to save the state. Because, carefully taking everything into account, he will discover that something which appears to be a virtue, if pursued, will result in his ruin; while some other thing which seems to be a vice, if pursued, will secure his safety and his well being.

The Prince, XV

Niccolò Machiavelli was a realist; a political thinker who believed that accurate knowledge of political life is the necessary condition for political success. However, his style of political thinking can be better described as a refined realism, which encompasses some intellectual features normally associated with political idealism and even political prophecy.

Machiavelli believed that studying political reality is worthier than imagining abstract models for good principalities or republics, although he admired Plato and Aristotle, who wrote of imagined republics because they were animated by a passion for true glory (*OW*, i.115). In Machiavelli's view, human beings judge political matters by looking at leaders' real accomplishments: 'In the actions of all men, and especially of princes, where there is no tribunal to which to appeal, one must consider the final result,' he states in *The Prince* (*P*, XVIII). In the *Discourses*, when he analyses the Gracchi's struggle in the first century BC to introduce agrarian laws aimed at attenuating the plebs' poverty, he remarks that their efforts provoked harsh resentment within the Roman nobility and led to the collapse of republican liberty. For this reason, their actions cannot be praised, and their example must not be followed, even if their intention was laudable (*D*, I.37). Machiavelli knew that political leaders frequently make lethal mistakes on the basis of an inadequate knowledge of political life and history. The wise Cicero made the error of sending Octavian, the nephew of Caesar, to fight Mark Antony, hoping that Mark Antony's soldiers would desert him for Caesar's successor. But Mark Antony made an alliance with Octavian that led to the complete isolation of Cicero and the Senate. 'Cicero should have known better,' Machiavelli remarks, 'that from Caesar's successors or followers nothing in favour of liberty could have come' (*D*, I.52).

While he was always a severe critic of imprudent leaders who underestimated the risks of their actions, he also deplored postponing decisions, for fear of being too rash and too bold. For Machiavelli, indecisiveness is a typical sign of weakness: 'irresolute republics never take up good policies unless by force, because their weakness never allows them to decide where there is any doubt; and if that doubt is not suppressed by violence that drives them on, they always remain in suspense' (*D*, I.38). The choice is not between daring or caution, but between a political conduct that is in tune with the context, and a political conduct that is not. In chaotic, dangerous times a normally insane political decision is in fact the right choice to make. In his letter of

September 1506 to Giovan Battista Soderini, Machiavelli states that different modes of action may lead to the same results, whereas identical modes of action can produce opposite outcomes. Scipio succeeded in Spain by governing his army with mildness and personal integrity. Hannibal succeeded in Italy by displaying the most inhumane cruelty against his own soldiers. Had Scipio used Hannibal's methods in Spain, he would have failed. Hannibal, in turn, would have failed had he behaved like Scipio. The key is to act as the times and the mood of peoples require. From this perspective, Machiavelli's manner of thinking is different from other kinds of realism: he has a mature awareness that the necessary condition for successful political action, even the most innovative, is the ability to read the moment.

Machiavelli also believed that at times 'rare and marvellous men' appear on the world's stage (perhaps sent by God) to accomplish grand things like unifying scattered peoples, emancipating nations, resurrecting political liberty. He was convinced that others like Moses, Cyrus, Theseus, and Romulus would emerge. In the final chapter of *The Prince*, having explained what a new prince should do to preserve a principality, he openly invokes a redeemer to liberate Italy from the barbarians. Such an extraordinary achievement would be possible, and indeed easy, because the times were ripe. No other political writer has combined the strictest adherence to political reality with the most powerful political imagination.

Machiavelli's friend Francesco Guicciardini judged that his realism was tainted by idealism. Ten years younger than Machiavelli, a member of one of the wealthiest and most powerful families of Florence, cold, prudent, ambitious, Guicciardini was able to occupy a number of very prestigious positions, including that of governor of the papal states of Modena and Reggio. Guicciardini knew Machiavelli well and appreciated his integrity, his total devotion to the cause of the liberation of Italy from foreign domination, and his irresistible humour. In spite of his admiration, Guicciardini did not consider him a true realist.

For him Machiavelli was a political thinker too keen to generalize and to interpret political reality through abstract models and examples from antiquity. With subtle irony, in a letter of 18 May 1521, Guicciardini reproached Machiavelli for discussing general forms of government like monarchy, aristocracy and republic rather than restricting himself to the analysis of contingent political situations. He also remarked that it was a mistake to cite the example of the ancient Romans, as Machiavelli did so many times in *The Prince*, in the *Discourses* and in *The Art of War*, because each situation is unique. Political decisions should be taken by using discretion, a highly refined form of political prudence that is not based on general rules, cannot be learned in books, and which very few men have by nature or are able to attain through long practice.

Machiavelli, on the contrary, was keen to suggest highly imaginative and risky courses of political action. During the dramatic political and military crisis of 1525–7, which led to the sack of Rome, he suggested that the peoples of Romagna be armed and subject to papal dominion, following his general principle that armies composed of citizens, or subjects, do better than mercenary troops. While an imaginative idea, those subjects were profoundly divided and hostile to the prince they were supposed to fight for. Not surprisingly, Guicciardini and the Pope did not approve Machiavelli's plan, even if they saw its merit. In this specific case Machiavelli was too bold. However, in general, his capacity for imagining new political strategies was his main virtue, and not, as Guicciardini believed, his vice. Men like Pope Clement VII and Guicciardini were not able, with all their realism, to save Italy from falling under the most ignominious foreign domination.

Machiavelli also maintained that the power of words plays a role in political life. In *The Art of War* he stresses the importance of eloquence and lists rhetorical skills as one of the essential features of a good general: 'To persuade or dissuade a few of a thing is very easy. For if words are not enough, you can then use authority or force. But the difficulty is in removing from a multitude a sinister opinion that is also contrary either to the common good or to your opinion. There one can use only words that are heard by all, wishing to persuade all of them together.' Held in the greatest respect by ancient generals, oratory has become in modern times obsolete, Machiavelli sadly remarks. Yet, nothing is more effective than eloquence to impel an army's will, and to move the soldiers' passions: 'For infinite times things arise by means of which an army falls to ruin, when the captain either does not know or is not used to speaking to it. For this speaking takes away fear, inflames spirits, increase obstinacy, uncovers deceptions, promises rewards, shows dangers and the way to flee them, fills with hope, praises, vituperates, and does all of those things by which the human passions are extinguished or inflamed' (*AW*, IV.137–41). Machiavelli concludes that a captain of any new military establishment must know how to speak to his soldiers. He is aware that eloquence alone will not preserve states. It is 'easy to persuade peoples,' he writes in *The Prince*, but it is 'difficult to keep them persuaded'. For this reason 'all armed prophets succeed whereas unarmed ones fail'. He cites Girolamo Savonarola, who 'perished together with his new political orders as soon as the masses began to lose faith in him; and he lacked the means of keeping the support of those who had believed in him, as well as of making those who had never had any faith in him believe'. A true political leader must be able 'to force them to believe', as Moses, Cyrus, Theseus and Romulus did (*P*, VI). Still, the power of words has always helped the attainment of great political deeds, and a serious political realist must take into account the power of rhetoric just as it must recognize military and economic power.

Machiavelli believed that only the refined interpretation of a political situation can in part, and tentatively, unveil political reality. For this reason his realism must not be confused with the realism of the empirical scientist who collects precise facts and identifies general laws. Yet many scholars regard Machiavelli as one of the founders of the modern science of politics; they stress that he found regular or recurrent features in the human world that form the basis of general laws of politics. They cite a passage from the *Discourses*: 'Prudent men are accustomed to say, and not by chance or without merit, that whoever wishes to see what has to be considers what has been: for all worldly things in every time have their own counterpart in ancient times. That arises because these are the work of men, who have and always had the same passions, and they must of necessity result in the same effect' (*D*, III.43). Yet Machiavelli's belief in the sameness of human passions over history, a common theme in the early sixteenth century, did not lead to the scientific study of politics but to an interpretive work aimed at understanding the specific features of political life and events, attempting predictions, offering practical advice, and writing historical narratives based upon the identification of the political actors' intentions. Even if he believed that men have and have always had the same passions, Machiavelli also knew that each individual has *his* own passions and temperament, and acts accordingly. 'I believe,' he wrote to Giovan Battista Soderini, 'that as nature has given each man an individual face, so she has given him an individual disposition and an individual imagination. From this it results that each man conducts himself according to his disposition and his imagination' (*L*, 399). To predict political behaviour, one must identify the particular disposition and imagination of individual actors.

This difficult task requires a political adviser to be 'there' or at least 'close' to the events and to peoples, and to collect and review facts and information. The clouds that surround political action, however, never go away because of the deception of political actors (who deceive themselves, at times). The interpretive work is valuable, but hardly conclusive; the best one can hope for is to come up with plausible advice that will join the counsel of other advisors. Judgements about men's actions, and particularly princes' actions, can never be final because, as Machiavelli remarks, there is no judge to whom one can appeal for a conclusive verdict (*P*, XVIII). In political life, the 'truth of the matter' must often be uncovered by decoding theatrical performances that princes stage in order to impress and scare their subjects as well as their enemies. One example that Machiavelli cites is the murder of Remirro de Orco by the Duke Cesare Borgia. In chapter 7 of *The Prince* Machiavelli reports the episode as a harsh but necessary measure to allay the subjects' hatred. He also emphasizes the efficacy of the staging: 'because he [the Duke] recognized that the severe measures that had been taken had resulted in his becoming hated by some people, in order to dispel this ill-feeling and win everyone to him, he wanted to show that if any cruel deeds had been committed they were attributable to the harshness of his government, not to himself. And availing himself of an appropriate opportunity, one morning the Duke had Remirro placed in two pieces in the square at Cesena, with a block of wood and a bloodstained sword at his side. This terrible spectacle left the people both satisfied and amazed.' Machiavelli registers the power of the performance over the subjects, but some thirteen years earlier, when he saw the scene in Cesena, he had written to the Signoria in Florence that by placing the body of Remirro in the square cut 'in two pieces', the duke made it clear that he had complete power over bodies, political and individual: just as he was able to turn the dismembered Romagna into a unified political body, he was also capable of dismembering Remirro's body.[2] As the comparison of the two descriptions of the same event makes clear, Machiavelli was a realist capable of interpreting the same fact in different manners.

Machiavelli regarded the knowledge of political reality to be the essential requisite for effective political action, whatever the goals that political leaders want to attain, and he also explained that in all times and all places historians and ordinary people ('volgo') judge political leaders on the basis of the effective results of their actions. In addition to that he insisted on a strong and reliable military power for every state. These elements of his political thought do situate him at the centre of the long tradition of political realism. Yet, he was able to imagine political possibilities that were very remote from reality (if not impossible), such as the resurrection of republican governments to replace principalities and monarchies and the unification and independence of Italy. Not only did he believe that they could indeed become real, but he devoted his best energies to making them become real. For him political reality was made of many elements: passions, interests, intentions, ability to simulate and dissimulate. More than a system of facts, it was a world of uncertain and ambivalent signs, words and gestures, accessible, only in part, through a work of interpretation. He knew that political reality is extremely difficult to grasp, and believed that the true realist, and the true political leader, is a person who is able to imagine new and better worlds and manners of living, and to work, with determination and prudence, to making them real.

3

THE LION AND THE FOX

How praiseworthy it is for a prince to keep his word and to live with integrity and not by cunning everyone knows. Nevertheless, one sees from experience in our times that the princes who have accomplished great deeds are those who have thought little about keeping faith and who have known how to manipulate cunningly men's minds; and in the end, they have surpassed those who laid their foundations upon sincerity.

Therefore, you must know that there are two modes of fighting: one with the laws, the other with force. The first is proper to man, the second to beasts. But because the first, in many cases, is not sufficient, it becomes necessary to have recourse to the second: therefore, a prince must know how to use well the natures of both the beast and the man. This rule was taught to princes symbolically by the writers of antiquity: they recounted how Achilles and many others of those ancient princes were given to Chiron the Centaur to be raised and cared for under his discipline. This can only mean that having a half-beast and half-man as a teacher, a prince must know how to employ the nature of the one and the other; for the one without the other is not lasting.

Since, then, a prince must know how to use well the nature of the beast, he should choose from among the beasts the fox and the lion; for the lion cannot defend itself from traps, while the fox cannot protect itself from the wolves. It is therefore necessary to be a fox, in order to recognize the traps, and a lion, in order to frighten the wolves: those who base their behaviour only on the lion do not understand things. A wise ruler, therefore, cannot and should not keep his word when such an observance would be to his disadvantage and when the reasons that caused him to make a promise are removed. If men were all good, this precept would not be good. But since men are a wicked lot and will not keep their promises to you, you likewise need not keep yours to them. A prince never lacks legitimate reasons to colour over his failure to keep his word. Of this, one could cite an endless number of modern examples to show how many pacts and how many promises have been made null and void because of the faithlessness of princes; and he who has known best how to use the ways of the fox has come out best. But it is necessary to know how to colour this nature well and to be a great pretender and dissembler. Men are so simple-minded and so controlled by their immediate necessities that he who deceives will always find someone who will let himself be deceived.

The Prince, *XVIII*

This famous passage from *The Prince* has been read over the centuries as compelling evidence that Machiavelli emancipated politics from ethics and initiated a way of thinking, and acting, which amounts to a radical break with previous classical and Christian ways of interpreting politics. This view, which scholars have called at times 'the autonomy of politics' or the concept of 'dirty hands', is in part correct, but it does not allow us to properly understand Machiavelli's conception of political action and life. What he intended to accomplish in *The Prince* and in all his political works was to correct the weaknesses of classical and Christian theories, not to reject them altogether. Like classical political thinkers, in particular Cicero, he stressed that true political action requires the practice of political virtues; like Christian political writers he maintained that God favours the great men who are capable of founding and preserving good political orders. However, he interpreted in a new manner the concept of political virtue and God's favour.

To appreciate the true sense of Machiavelli's ideas, we must first of all consider what his fellow Florentines thought of political action. Politics, or civil science, was praised as the most noble of all intellectual endeavours, while the word 'state' had, as we shall see, a dubious connotation. In early-sixteenth-century Florence, public rhetoric, philosophy and historiography was still influenced by the Aristotelian and Ciceronian interpretation of politics, which believed in preserving and reforming a community of free and equal citizens living together for the common good under the rule of law and understanding the civil man as an upright citizen who serves the common good with justice, prudence, fortitude and temperance. The founder of Florentine political rhetoric was Brunetto Latini, who presented politics as the highest among the humane practical arts and the most noble activity of man, because its aim is to teach how to rule the inhabitants of a kingdom, and a people, in times of both peace and war, according to reason and justice.[3]

The classical conception of politics as the proper exercise of reason to ensure the rule of fair law became a common principle in sixteenth-century Florence. Coluccio Salutati, the great humanist and statesman, wrote that politics and law are one and the same thing.[4] He speaks of 'political reason' as a synonym of the 'civil reason'.[5] Politics' goal is the good citizen; so is the legislator's.[6] Their concern is the order of the city and the whole of humanity. For Salutati, politics is responsible for the health of the soul, and for men's happiness. Only politics, through law, makes political or civil felicity available to men by creating the conditions for a virtuous life.

The logical corollary of this interpretation was that politics deserves the highest status among human sciences and arts, another conventional theme of Florentine public rhetoric. Leonardo Bruni, one of the towering figures of Florentine humanism, explained this point in the 'Proem' to his translation of Aristotle's *Politics*. The republic is a self-governing community where the common good prevails over particular interests, and only in such a community can individuals enjoy happiness and a truly human life. A civil society where men are self-sufficient and have a strong moral life is the most precious common good. Therefore, Bruni remarks, the art that teaches what a civil society is, and how it is to be preserved, deserves the highest rank among human disciplines.[7]

The celebration of politics continued as part of Florentine intellectual life in the second half of the Quattrocento. However, even if they endorsed this elevated conception, Florentine citizens and political leaders were aware that real political life is often dishonourable. The records of the debates of advisory bodies attended by members of the Florentine elite indicate their awareness that the security of the Republic can violate the principles of justice and law. In the meeting summoned to debate the treason of the military condottiere, Paolo Vitelli – at which Machiavelli was present – the issue to be decided was whether Vitelli ought or not to be treated 'according to reason', that is according to justice and the law.[8] As one of the speakers remarks, since it would be dangerous for the Republic to leave Vitelli alive, in his case one 'should not proceed according to the precepts of reason'. To justify violating the rule of justice, the speaker appeals to the usual practice of states: matters of state, he says, are not to be handled according to reason.[9] By the beginnings of the second decade of the century, the conflict between moral and legal reason, and the interest of the state, began to be described not as a divergence between reason and the practice of the state, but as a conflict between moral and legal reason and the 'reason of the state'.

The term 'reason of state' appears for the first time in Francesco Guicciardini's *Dialogue of the Government of Florence*, composed between 1521 and 1524. Citing the example of the Genoese, who did not release the prisoners they captured at the battle of Meloria in 1284, thereby inflicting an irreparable blow on their Pisan enemies, Bernardo del Nero argues that what the Genoese did was a cruelty of which moral conscience can never approve. However, since all states – with the sole exception of republics within their own territory – are grounded on nothing but sheer violence, to preserve them it is necessary to resort to violence again and again. Bernardo del Nero concludes, 'When I talked of murdering or keeping the Pisans imprisoned, I didn't perhaps talk as a Christian: I talked according to the reason and practice of states.'[10] He then says that 'anyone who doesn't acknowledge this has no excuse before God because – as the friars like to say – it shows "crass ignorance"'. One must choose either to follow God's law and remove oneself from the world of politics, or remain in the world of politics, and violate God's law.

Machiavelli acknowledged the value of the realists' argument, but defended the classical conception of political action, even its excellence in God's eyes. He achieves this remarkable intellectual feat by first submitting the principles of prevailing political rhetoric (based above all upon the teaching of Cicero and Christianity) to a realist critique. In Cicero's immensely influential treatise *Of Duties*, we read that a ruler can attain honour only if he avoids wrongdoing 'either by force or by fraud': 'Fraud seems to belong to the cunning fox, force to the lion. Both ways of fighting are wholly unworthy of man, even if fraud is the more contemptible' (*Of Duties*, I.13.41). Machiavelli's reply, as shown in the passage that opens this chapter, was that the prince must imitate both the fox and the lion to attain security and honour.

Cicero also maintained that 'of all the motives, none is better adapted to secure influence and hold it fast than love; nothing is more foreign to that end than fear'. From this principle he had derived a straightforward piece of advice: 'let us, then, embrace this policy, which appeals to every heart and is the strongest support not only of security but also of influence and power – namely to banish fear and cleave to love. And thus we shall most easily secure success both in private and in public life' (*Of Duties*,

II.7.24). On this subject too Machiavelli rejects Cicero's views. Since men are, he writes, 'ungrateful, fickle, feigners and dissemblers, avoiders of danger, eager for gain, while you benefit them they are all devoted to you: they would shed their blood for you; they offer their possessions, their lives, and their sons, as I said before, when the need to do so is far off. But when you are hard pressed, they turn away'. In Machiavelli's view it is better that princes be feared than loved, if one cannot be both, because 'men are less hesitant about offending or harming a ruler who makes himself loved than one who inspires fear' (*P*, XVII). Last, Cicero had proclaimed that 'no cruelty can be expedient; for cruelty is most abhorrent to human nature, whose lead we ought to follow'. Machiavelli responds that there are cruelties that 'may be called well committed (if one may use the word "well" of that which is evil) when they are all committed at once, because they are necessary for establishing one's power, and are not afterwards persisted in, but changed for measures as beneficial as possible to one's subjects' (*P*, VIII). Even if 'every ruler should want to be thought merciful', not cruel, one should nonetheless take care 'not to be merciful in an inappropriate way', and be able to use cruelty well (*P*, XVIII).

Machiavelli's argument is that Ciceronian and Christian rules of morality are to be followed except in situations of necessity. The use of fraud is always 'detestable'; yet 'in the conduct of a war is praiseworthy and glorious'. A fraud which involves breaking your word or the contracts you have made is not glorious at all: 'for, although on occasion it may win for you a state or a kingdom...it will never bring you glory'. What turns a fraud into a praiseworthy and glorious deed is that a prince or a ruler uses it 'with an enemy who has not kept faith with you, i.e., a fraud which is involved in the conduct of war' (*D*, III.40). The same applies to cruelties, injustices, simulation, deceit; in brief, to all the derogations of virtue.

Romulus, the legendary founder of Rome, killed his brother then consented to the death of Titus Tatius the Sabine, chosen by him as a partner in the kingdom. He can be excused for his crime because the end was good. In a similar case, Machiavelli writes that the actions of the Spartan king Cleomenes – who 'had all the ephors and anyone else who might be able to stand against him killed' because he realized that he could not restore the laws of Lycurgus 'unless he alone were in authority' – were 'just and praiseworthy' (D, I.9). He only excuses Romulus, rather than praising him like Cleomenes, because Romulus's crime was too enormous to be entirely justified. Machiavelli goes as far as to write that 'a prince must be prudent enough to know how to escape the infamy of those vices that would take the state away from him, and be on guard against those vices that will not take it from him, whenever possible. But if he cannot, he need not concern himself unduly if he ignores these less serious vices. Moreover, he need not worry about incurring the infamy of those vices without which it would be difficult to save the state. Because, carefully taking everything into account, he will discover that something which appears to be a virtue, if pursued, will result in his ruin; while some other thing which seems to be a vice, if pursued, will secure his safety and his well being' (P, XV).

His wording is precise. Next he writes that a man who wants 'always to act honourably' will inevitably fall because he is surrounded by many unscrupulous men; therefore, 'it is necessary for a prince, if he wants to maintain his power, to learn to be able not to be good and to use it [the capacity to be not good] or not to use it according to necessity'. A few lines later he restates the same point in even clearer terms: 'I know that everyone will acknowledge that it would be most praiseworthy for a ruler to have all the above mentioned qualities that are held to be good. But because the reality of human life does not permit it, it is necessary to know how to avoid becoming notorious for those vices that would destroy one's power and seek to avoid those vices that are not politically dangerous.' As long as a prince or a ruler is able, he must not 'deviate from right conduct'; but he must 'be capable of entering upon the path of wrongdoing, if forced by necessity', or to better render his wording, 'necessitated' (*P*, XVIII).

Even if he presents his advice as universal truth, Machiavelli was well aware that in real political life all rules of conduct must be adapted to specific circumstances. For instance, the rule 'it is much better to be feared than to be loved' is subject to many exceptions. As Machiavelli notices in *Discourses* III.20, 'here it is to be considered with this true example how much more a humane act full of charity is sometimes able to do in the spirits of men than a ferocious and violent act, and that *often* those provinces and those cities that arms, warlike instruments, and every other human force have not been able to open have been opened by one example of humanity and of mercy, of chastity or of liberality'. Contrary examples aside, what makes the rule highly tentative is that its effectiveness depends on the virtue of the prince or captain who puts it into practice, that is on a completely contingent element. Princes and captains make serious mistakes, Machiavelli remarks, either when they make themselves loved too much, or when they make themselves feared too much: 'for he who desires too much to be loved becomes despicable, however little he departs from the true way; the other, who desires too much to be feared, becomes hateful, however little he exceeds the mode' (*D*, III.21). What makes the rule an effective truth is the virtue of the political leader, his capacity to put the rule into practice according to the specific circumstances within which he is operating, as well as his personal reputation. It is the virtue of the commander which mitigates the excessive desire to be feared or the excessive desire to be loved, and 'properly seasons' every mode of life. Machiavelli's general rules of political conduct are therefore not only subject to many counter-examples and exceptions, but also require a substantial work of temperament and adaptation.

At the same time, and this is the aspect of Machiavelli's teaching that almost all scholars have failed to notice, he argues that a prince who enters in evil to found new and good political orders can count on God's friendship. He supported his innovative interpretation of Christian political ethics with biblical examples, recounting the episode of David, who refused to use the armour that King Saul had offered him to stress that a wise prince must employ his own and not somebody else's armies (*P*, XIII). Moreover, Machiavelli asserts that princes who use cruelties well 'can remedy their standing both with God and with men' (*P*, VIII). His greatest political hero, after all, was Moses, a friend of God who accomplished the extraordinary work of leading an enslaved people to their emancipation. But Moses, so the Bible tells us in Exodus, ordered on behalf of God the extermination of a great number of Israelites who had worshipped the golden calf, and it is not even clear that God had authorized Moses to issue that cruel order. Machiavelli's *Prince* then was both a critique of Ciceronian political ethics, and a rejection of conventional Christian political teaching. To the first he proposed a new description of true political virtue which ensures security and honour; to the second an unconventional interpretation of God's attitude to founders and political leaders.

4

GOD'S FRIENDSHIP AND LOVE OF COUNTRY

Therefore, considering all of the things discussed above and thinking to myself whether at present in Italy the times are suitable to honour a new prince, and if there is the material that might give a prudent and virtuous prince the opportunity to introduce a form that would do him honour and bring benefit to the people of Italy, it seems to me that so many circumstances are favourable to such a new prince that I know of no other time more appropriate to this. And if, as I said, it was necessary for the people of Israel to be enslaved in Egypt to recognize the virtue of Moses, and it was necessary for the Persians to be oppressed by the Medes to recognize the greatness of spirit in Cyrus, and it was necessary for the Athenians to be scattered to recognize the excellence of Theseus, then, at present, to recognize the virtue of an Italian spirit, it was necessary for Italy to be reduced to her present conditions and that she be more enslaved than the Hebrews, more servile than the Persians, more scattered than the Athenians: without a leader, without order, beaten, despoiled, ripped apart, overrun, and having suffered every sort of ruin.

And even though before now, some glimmer of light may have shown itself in a single individual, so that it was possible to believe that God had ordained him for Italy's redemption, yet it was afterwards seen how at the height of his deeds, he was rejected by Fortune. Now, Italy, left as if lifeless, awaits the man who may heal her wounds and put an end to the plundering of Lombardy, the extortions in the Kingdom of Naples and in Tuscany, and who can cure her of those sores that have been festering for so long a time. Look how she now prays to God to send someone to redeem her from these barbaric cruelties and insults. See how ready and willing she is to follow a banner, provided that someone picks it up. Nor is there anyone in sight, at present, in whom she can have more hope than in Your Illustrious House, which, with its fortune and virtue, favoured by God and by the Church, of which it is now prince, could place itself at the head of this redemption. This will not be very difficult if you keep before your eyes the deeds and the lives of those named above. Although those men were rare and marvellous, they were nevertheless men, and each of them had less opportunity than the present one, for their undertakings were no more just, nor easier than this one, nor was God more a friend to them than to you. This is a righteous cause: 'iustum enim est bellum quibus necessarium et pia arma ubi nulla nisi in armis spes est' ['Only those wars that are necessary are just, and arms are sacred when there is no hope except through arms']. Here, circumstances are very favourable, and where circumstances are favourable, there cannot be great difficulty provided that you imitate the institutions of those men I have proposed as your target. Besides this, we now see here extraordinary, unprecedented signs brought about by God: the sea has opened up; a cloud has shown you the path; the rock has poured water forth; here, manna has rained; everything has converged for your greatness. The rest you must do yourself. God does not wish to do everything, in order not to take our free will from us and part of the glory that is ours.

The Prince, *XXVI*

Machiavelli was born and grew up in a city where eloquence was regarded as a noble art and a necessary skill for citizens in government. The statutes of the Studio Fiorentino issued by

Florence's University state that eloquence is the 'highest ornament of political life'. Angelo Poliziano, one of the leading
figures of Florentine culture, said in his opening lecture on rhetoric in 1480 that it was the necessary component of the
education of a civil man. Nothing is more beautiful, Poliziano
explains, than to distinguish oneself in the very art that makes
men excellent over other animals; nothing is more marvellous
than to penetrate the mind and soul of a multitude, to captivate
the people's attention, to drive their will and dominate their passions. Eloquence permits us to embellish and celebrate virtuous
men and their actions, and to darken the wicked; to persuade
one's fellow citizens to pursue what is useful for the common
good and avoid what is damaging and malignant. Eloquence is
the breastplate and the sword with which we defend ourselves
and the common good against our enemies and the enemies of
the Republic. Thanks to eloquent men, Poliziano remarks, states
have obtained the greatest advantages, and for this reason oratory
has in all times been rewarded and held in the highest honour.[11]
All Florentine political writers of the fifteenth and sixteenth centuries took Latin theorists of eloquence, particularly Cicero and
Quintilian, as their masters. From their texts they learned that
the good orator must conclude with the exhortation; that his last
words must be particularly effective. Of all passions, the most
powerful are indignation and pity. To excite indignation he must
magnify, with the right words, images, similes and metaphors,
the cruelty, ambitions and wickedness of the person or the state
he wants his audience or readers to act against; to excite compassion, he must magnify the innocence, the helplessness, the
sufferance of the victim.

Machiavelli masterfully applies this basic rule of political oratory in *The Prince*. He ends his text with a powerful exhortation
to emancipate Italy from foreign domination, stressing the cruelties and the insolences that the barbarians have inflicted upon
Italy, and stimulates compassion by pointing to Italy's weakness
and helplessness: 'more enslaved than the Hebrews, more

servile than the Persians, more scattered than the Athenians, without a leader, without order, beaten, despoiled, ripped apart, overrun, and having suffered every sort of ruin'. These are words that move the listener, and express Machiavelli's strong feelings about Italy's emancipation. Unlike most contemporary writers, he was envisaging Italy's unification and independence as the most pressing political goal of his time.

Machiavelli also argues that the deed is possible. Although the great redeemers of peoples were rare and marvellous men, 'they were nevertheless men'. Their deeds can be imitated. Moreover, Machiavelli promises a future redeemer God's friendship and help, as God helped Moses. This bold claim rests for him upon his conviction that God loves founders of political orders more than any other men. In another oration composed in 1520 to encourage constitutional reform in Florence, he states: 'I believe that the greatest honour men can receive is one that is given voluntarily by their country. And I believe the greatest good one can do, and the most acceptable to God, is the good one does for one's country' (*OW*, I.115). God loves political founders and reformers, because they are, like him, creators of lasting and beautiful orders. For this reason he rewards them with his friendship, and helps them to attain their goal. When Machiavelli guaranteed God's friendship, he was accomplishing a fine rhetorical move with a strong intellectual basis. The principle that God donates his friendship to those men who work for a just cause on earth came directly from the Bible and was one of the main tenets of Florentine civic religion. No other goal, he forcefully asserts in the 'Exhortation', is more just than to take up arms to emancipate Italy. Because the goal and the means are just, a redeemer of Italy would have God on his side and the goal would become possible.

Machiavelli's 'Exhortation' expressed his sincere patriotic passion and inspired Italian patriots who fought for national independence. Writing in 1827, Lord Macaulay said that although it is scarcely possible to read *The Prince* 'without horror and amazement', 'we are acquainted with few writings which exhibit so much elevation of sentiment, so pure and warm zeal for the public good...as those of Machiavelli'. His 'patriotic wisdom', Macaulay concludes, offered an oppressed people 'the last chance of emancipation and revenge'.[12] When Macaulay was writing these lines, the Italians were beginning to claim Machiavelli as the prophet of their independence and national unity. Carlo Cattaneo, one of the best minds of Italian Risorgimento, wrote that Machiavelli, who had been for three centuries the 'remorse of the conscience of unarmed Italy', had become the symbol of a people which at last was resolved to recover its dignity.[13] Cattaneo meant to say that Machiavelli was the only political thinker who had pointed to Italy's military weakness as the cause of its political servitude to Spain and France. When Italians were able in the nineteenth century to form respectable armies composed of Italian nationals, they were putting into practice what Machiavelli had taught three centuries before.

Love of country and zeal for the common good were for Machiavelli one and the same. He explicitly affirms the equation in the *Discourses*, where he writes that a prudent founder who intends to serve not his own interest but the common good, not the interests of his own successors but the common fatherland, must be alone in his authority. For him, like all republican political theorists, love of country is the passion which drives citizens to put the common good before personal and particular interests, to behave as a virtuous citizen in the proper sense. He describes the deeds of kings, captains and lawgivers who have laboured for their country as 'most virtuous' (*D*, I.Preface). He also equates fatherland ('patria') with republic, as opposed to principality and tyranny. In the *Discourses* he says that to conspire against the fatherland is to conspire against a republic, to become prince or tyrant of it and to usurp the legitimate political authority (*D*, III.6).

For Machiavelli love of country is a moral force that encourages its citizens to pursue the common good. In the *Discourses* he

comments upon Livy's account of the story of Manlius
Capitolinus, who was ordered by the tribunes of the plebs to
appear before the Roman people to defend his actions against
the Senate and the laws of the country. In Machiavelli's description, both the nobles and the tribunes behaved in a remarkably
virtuous way: the former did not support Manlius at all, even
though he was one of them and they 'were usually very keen to
defend one another'; the latter referred him to the judgement of
the popular assembly, even if Manlius had been inimical to the
Senate and they were always looking with favour to citizens who
opposed the nobles. But the most noteworthy feature of the
story is the behaviour of the Roman people. In spite of their
great desire to promote their interests and their hostility against
the nobles, they sentenced Manlius to death. 'With all of them' –
Machiavelli comments – 'love of country counted more than any
other consideration, and they looked upon the present dangers
for which he was responsible as of much greater importance than
his former merits; with the result that they chose he should die
in order that they might remain free' (D, III.8).

Machiavelli's interpretation of love of country as a compas-
sionate love of the common good is also evident when he writes
about Livy's account of Fabius Massimus Rullianus in the chapter of the *Discourses* entitled 'That a Good Citizen out of Love of
his Country ought to ignore Personal Affronts'. The Roman
Senate, Machiavelli explains, sent ambassadors to beseech Fabio
Massimo Rulliano to put his resentment aside and, for the
common good, to appoint Papirio Cursore dictator. 'Moved by
love of country', Fabio accepted the Senate's appeal, even though
he made it clear by his silence that the promotion of his adver-
sary was very painful for him. Machiavelli not only uses the term
'compassion' ('carità') to describe love of country, but he uses
again 'fatherland' and 'public good' as interchangeable terms to
show what inspires the patriot's conduct.

Machiavelli applies the classical conception of love of country
to modern politics. Although the history of Florence is the tri-

umph of ambition, factionalism, greed, envy, Florence too had examples of good citizens standing against tyranny and corruption for love of country. The orations Machiavelli attributes to anonymous citizens in the *Florentine Histories* are not historical documents, but embellished texts that reveal how Machiavelli believed a patriot should speak and act in momentous occasions of the life of the republic. An example is the anonymous citizens who spoke with great eloquence to halt the factional strife between the two powerful Florentine families of the Ricci and the Albizzi. Many citizens, Machiavelli writes, 'moved by love of their fatherland convened in the church of San Pietro in Scheraggio, and after much discussion, resolved to meet with the Signoria. One of them addressed the Signoria saying that it was "the love that we bear for our fatherland" that made them resolve to help to eliminate factional strife. He urges the Signori to introduce the political reform that would put an end to sects and restore "the free and civil life"'. The oration, Machiavelli notes, was the kind of speech that a good citizen 'moved by charity for [their] fatherland, not by any private passion', ought to deliver in times of cruel and devastating factional strife (*FH*, III.5).

Love of country was Machiavelli's deepest and lasting passion. At times the main object of his love was Florence; at other times Italy. In one of his last letters, written on 16 April 1527, he confessed that he loved his country more than his soul. The salvation of his country was for him more important than his own salvation. However, he also believed that by serving his country he was saving his soul, and that God granted perennial glory in heaven to those men who gave their souls for their country.

5

LEARNING FROM THE ANCIENTS

Considering thus how much honour is awarded to antiquity, and how many times – letting pass infinite other examples – a fragment of an ancient statue has been bought at a high price because someone wants to have it near oneself, to honour his house with it, and to be able to have it imitated by those who delight in that art and how the latter then strive with all industry to represent it in all their works; and seeing, on the other hand, that the most virtuous works the histories show us, which have been done by ancient kingdoms and republics, by kings, captains, citizens, legislators, and others who have laboured for their fatherland, are rather admired than imitated – indeed they are so much shunned by everyone in every least thing that no sign of that ancient virtue remains with us – I can do no other than marvel and grieve. And so much the more when I see that in the differences that arise between citizens in civil affairs or in the sicknesses that men incur, they always have recourse to those judgements or those remedies that were judged or ordered by the ancients. For the civil laws are nothing other than the verdicts given by the ancient jurists, which, reduced to order, teach our present jurists to judge. Nor is medicine other than the experiments performed by ancient physicians, on which present physicians found their judgements. Nonetheless, in ordering republics, maintaining states, governing kingdoms, ordering the military and administering war, judging subjects, and increasing empire, neither prince, nor republic may be found that has recourse to the example of the ancients. This arises, I believe, not so much from the weakness into which the present religion has led the world, or from the evil that an ambitious idleness has done to many Christian provinces and cities, as from not having a true knowledge of histories, through not getting from reading them that sense nor tasting that flavour that they have in themselves. From this it arises that the infinite number who read them take pleasure in hearing of the variety of accidents contained in them without thinking of imitating them, judging that imitation is not only difficult but impossible – as if heaven, sun, elements, men had varied in motion, order, and power from what they were in antiquity. Wishing, therefore, to turn men from this error, I have judged it necessary to write on all those books of Titus Livy that have been not intercepted by the malignity of the times whatever I shall judge necessary for their greater understanding, according to knowledge of ancient and modern things, so that those who read these statements of mine can more easily draw from them that utility for which one should seek knowledge of histories. Although this enterprise may be difficult, nonetheless, aided by those who have encouraged me to accept this burden, I believe I can carry it far enough so that a short road will remain for another to bring it to the destined place.

Discourses on Livy, *Proem to Book I*

Machiavelli's political theory was based on history. It is only from the knowledge of past political events, he believed, that we can understand present circumstances and act upon them effectively. Once again Machiavelli was following the footsteps of classical Roman political thinkers and their humanist followers of the fifteenth century. History, Cicero writes, 'bears witness to the passing of the ages, sheds light upon reality, gives life to recollection and guidance to human existence, and brings tidings of ancient days'.[14] Quintilian expands the same point in the *Institutio*:

'history seems to repeat itself and the experience of the past is a valuable support to reason'. For this reason, the study of history is particularly suited to deliberative oratory, and the speeches delivered to the people and the opinions expressed in the senate provide precious examples of advice and dissuasion.[15] History arouses love of virtue through the narration of grand examples of antiquity, and for this reason it is much more valuable than philosophy: 'it is still more important that we should know and ponder continually all the noblest sayings and deeds that have been handed down to us from ancient times. And assuredly we shall nowhere find a larger or more remarkable store of these than in the records of our own country. Who will teach courage, justice, loyalty, self-control, simplicity and contempt of grief and pain better than men like Fabricius, Curius, Regulus, Decius, Mucius and countless others. For if the Greeks bear away the palm for moral precepts, Rome can produce more striking examples of moral performance, which is a far greater thing.'[16]

This advice of classical rhetoricians was taken up by fifteenth-century Florentine historians. In his preface to the *Istoria Fiorentina*, a work that Machiavelli knew well, Leonardo Bruni writes that to compose the history of the Florentine people is a most useful pursuit both for private and public purposes, because history allows us to know the deeds and deliberations of ancient peoples in different epochs; it makes us prudent and teaches us what we should do and what we should avoid.[17] And by placing before our eyes the examples of excellent men, it arouses our soul to pursue virtue.[18] The same themes are reiterated by Iacopo Bracciolini, in the Proem to the Italian translation of his father Poggio Bracciolini's *Istoria Fiorentina*, another major work of fifteenth-century Florentine culture. Histories, he remarks, permit us to know the lives of men and of peoples, the different views that ancient peoples discussed in their councils, their deliberations, the different costumes of republics, the various games of fortune and the events of war; therefore it helps us to deliberate what is useful for us and for our country.[19]

Political thinking and writing based on history has disappeared from later and above all contemporary political philosophy. Most contemporary political thinkers argue how just political institutions and policies ought to be based on principles defined by abstract thinking. They are not concerned with the practice of these principles. Contemporary leading theorists do not need to know past history, and almost never cite the past to understand the present or to reinforce their normative arguments. The reasons for this transition are many. The first is the concern, powerfully voiced by Thomas Hobbes in the seventeenth century, that history can provide us only with uncertain and disputable opinions. Only philosophy, and in particular a philosophy modelled on geometry and logic, can deliver solid truths about political principles. Another is the view, that has in Immanuel Kant its most authoritative champion, that a valid political and moral argument must be based upon rational considerations and not on its emotional appeal. Even if contemporary political theory has its merits, the dismissed humanistic and Machiavellian approach still allows us to better understand political reality, and persuades individuals to act politically.

Machiavelli believed that human history was cyclical, not progressive. Countries like ancient Rome, which had been for centuries powerful and free, were in the sixteenth century enslaved and utterly corrupt, whereas countries like France that were in antiquity divided, powerless and unfree, were united, powerful and free. The world had been the same over time, in the sense that there had been 'as much good as wicked in it'; but 'the wicked and the good', Machiavelli adds, 'vary from province to province' (D, II.Preface). The ancients were better than moderns at founding and preserving political orders and we ought to humbly learn from them.

Machiavelli also noted that governments go through cyclical transformation. Following the teachings of the Greek historian Polybius (c.200–c.118 BC), he believed that there are six forms of government – three of them, monarchy, aristocracy and republic, were good; the other three, tyranny, oligarchy and democracy, were bad. These alternate in a pattern of progress and decline: monarchy, tyranny; aristocracy, oligarchy; republic, democracy. Machiavelli writes at the outset of the *Discourses*, 'rarely do they return to the same government, for almost no republic can have so long a life as to be able to pass many times through these changes and remain on its feet. But indeed it happens that in its travails, a republic always lacking in counsel and forces becomes subject to a neighbouring state that is ordered better than it' (*D*, I.2).

Machiavelli also believed that the power of the heavens and other natural or occult forces severely limit human freedom of action: 'the star and the heaven go wandering, now high, now low, without any rest . . . likewise nothing on earth remains in the same condition always' (*OW*, II.757–8). Heavenly motions and humours influence human events: 'From this [heaven's motion] result peace and war; on this depend the hatreds among those whom one wall and one moat shut up together' (*OW*, II.758). The cycle of progress and decay depends on a power that governs human things: 'Virtue makes countries tranquil, and from Tranquillity, Leisure next emerges, and Leisure burns the town and villages. Then, after a country has for a time been subject to lawlessness, Virtue often returns to live there once again. Such a course the power which governs human things permits and requires, so that nothing beneath the sun ever will or can be firm. And it is and always has been and always will be, that evil follows after good, good after evil' (*OW*, II.763). If a modern thinker believes that humanity is free to build its own progressive destiny unconstrained by natural or supernatural power, then Machiavelli is not a modern thinker. History, however, has vindicated his conception, unless one is prepared to argue that the triumph of fascist and Nazi regimes in Europe, the Holocaust, communist regimes, and many other horrors of our times were also part of the progress of humanity.

Heavenly plans can in part be detected, Machiavelli claimed, through divinations, revelations or prodigies. Charles VIII's invasion of Italy in 1494 was predicted by Girolamo Savonarola. Machiavelli believed in celestial signs and on the divinations based upon them: 'the atmosphere', he writes, 'is full of intelligences who, endowed by the natural virtue of foreseeing future events and feeling compassion for men they warn them by means of such signs so that they may provide for the necessary defences' (*D*, I.56) – more evidence that it is an anachronism to read Machiavelli as a 'modern' man emancipated from magic conceptions of the world.

Heaven, Fortune and God populate Machiavelli's cosmos. Each has a role, though this is not well defined. Heaven presides over orderly motions, cycles of progress, decay, death, regeneration and corruption. It rules the course of all things in the world, and periodically purges nations and societies with pestilences, famines and flood: 'when nature has accumulated too much superfluous material, it frequently acts in the same way and by means of purges restores the health of the body'. Similar processes occur for Machiavelli in countries and states: 'when every province is replete with inhabitants who can neither obtain a livelihood nor move elsewhere since all other places are occupied and full up, and when the craftiness and malignity of man has gone as far as it can go, the world needs be purged in one of these three ways [pestilence, famine and flood], so that mankind, being reduced to comparatively few and humbled by adversity, may adopt a more appropriate form of life and grow better' (*D*, II.5).

Machiavelli imagines Fortune as the capricious and malignant goddess who takes pleasure in tormenting the good and rewarding the wicked. He describes her role, status and power in a poem. She has her own kingdom and from her throne governs the whole world and disposes of time as she pleases. Above the gates of her palace 'sit Luck and Chance, without eyes and without ears'; inside, she sits surrounded by wheels which never stop turning, day and night, 'because Heaven commands that Laziness and Necessity whirl them around'. She uses her immense power over the things of the world in a completely arbitrary way, 'without compassion, without law, without right'. She often 'keeps the good beneath her feet' and 'raises the wicked up', deprives the just of the good that she arbitrarily 'gives to the unjust', and often 'seats the undeserving on a throne to which the deserving never attains'.

For Machiavelli human beings can at best control half their actions. Whereas heaven presides over orderly and necessary motions, Fortune is the mistress of chance and accident. Her eyes are ferocious and sharp; she distinguishes the good, whom she punishes with servitude, infamy and sickness, and the audacious, 'who push, shove, and jostle her', whom she rewards with power, honour and riches. In a well-known passage of *The Prince*, Machiavelli maintains that 'it is better to be impetuous than cautious, because Fortune is a woman, and if you want to hold her down, it is necessary to beat her and to force her down. It is clear that she more often allows herself to be won over by impetuous men than by those who proceed coldly. And so, like a woman, Fortune is always the friend of young men, for they are less cautious, more ferocious, and they command her with more audacity' (*P*, XXV). However, not even the most brave and the most audacious, like Caesar and Alexander, can outstand her power or outwit her malignity: the former failed to reach 'the coveted harbor'; the latter 'covered with wounds, in his enemy's shadow was slain'. To really master her, men ought to be able to 'understand the times and the order of things and to adapt himself to them'. If they were able to do so, they 'would have always good fortune, or he would protect himself always from bad, and it would come true that the wise man would rule the stars and the Fates'. But since Heaven does not permit individuals to change their nature, 'Fortune varies and commands men and holds them under her yoke.'

When Fortune wants men to accomplish great things, she

chooses a man of high spirit and great virtue capable of seizing the occasion that she offers him; in like manner, when she wants to bring about a disaster for a country, she supports men who cause that ruin, and should anyone have the power to curtail its plan, 'it either kills him off or deprives him of all the power of doing good'. Hence, Machiavelli concludes, 'men may second fortune, but cannot oppose it'; 'they may weave its warp, but cannot break it'. It does not follow though that men should cease 'to sweat much over things' and let themselves be governed by fate. Men's virtue can resist her power; they can check it 'by means of dikes and dams'; by means of good political and military orders. Moreover, since Fortune always proceeds in unpredictable ways, we 'should never give up'; we 'should never despair', however hopeless and difficult are our circumstances.

For Machiavelli the proper guidance for political action can only come from knowledge of the past, as a source both of political wisdom and moral inspiration. He composed the *Discourses* to extract from history the political wisdom necessary to find new 'modes and new orders', and to promote the grand deeds of the ancient Romans.

Machiavelli maintains that, through historical examples, the orator can bring alive the horrors of corruption, ambition, vainglory avarice; he can touch the audience's feelings and imagination, not just their reason, and compel them to flee vice and follow virtue. If a prince reads ancient histories, Machiavelli writes, he will *see* the good emperors living in safety among safe citizens, 'a world full of peace and justice', the senate's authority respected, the magistrates honoured, rich citizens enjoying their wealth, nobility and virtue held in the highest esteem, the absence of any rancour, any licentiousness, corruption or ambition, the 'world in triumph', its prince glorious and respected by all, the people fond of him and secure under his rule. If then he reads the histories of bad emperors, he will *see* their times fraught with wars, torn by seditions, brutal alike in peace and in war, assassinations, civil wars and foreign wars, Italy abused and ever a prey to fresh misfortunes, its cities demolished and pillaged, Rome burnt, its Capitol demolished by its own citizens, ancient temples lying desolate, religious rites grown corrupt, adultery rampant, the sea covered with exiles and the rocks stained with blood, countless atrocities perpetrated, rank, riches, the honours men have won, and, above all, virtue looked upon as capital crimes, calumniators rewarded, servants suborned to turn against their masters, freed men to turn against their patrons, and those who lack enemies attacked by their friends.

Whereas in the *Discourses* Machiavelli comments on Livy's history, in the *Florentine Histories*, he writes his own. Like classical rhetoricians, he believes that 'if every example of a republic is moving, those which one reads concerning one's own are much more so and much more useful' (*FH*, Proem). He reports examples of corruption and ineptitude, claiming his history is valuable: 'even if in describing the things that happened in this corrupt world one does not tell about either the strength of the soldiers, or the virtue of the captain, or the love of the citizen for his fatherland, it will be seen with what deceits, with what guile and arts the princes, the soldiers, and head of republics conducted themselves so as to maintain the reputation they have not deserved. It may, perhaps, be no less useful to know these things than to know the ancient ones, because, if the latter excite liberal spirits to follow them, the former will excite such spirits to avoid and eliminate them' (*FH*, V.1). Histories of dark times are more useful than abstract reasoning, not only because they arouse emotions but also because they offer material for refined political wisdom. Machiavelli describes the civil strife and factions in Florence, and offers his compatriot useful advice on how to preserve the republican order from devastating conflicts: 'if no other lesson is useful to the citizens who govern republics, it is that which shows the causes of the hatred and divisions in the city, so that when they have become wise through the dangers of others, they may be able to maintain themselves united' (*FH*, Proem).

If political leaders of our times followed Machiavelli's belief that true political wisdom is based on knowledge of the past and not on abstract principles or models constructed by philosophers or social scientists, many devastating mistakes would have been avoided.

6

WAR AND GLORY

I want to begin from your words, where you said that in war, which is my art, I had not used any ancient means. About this I say that as this is an art by means of which men cannot live honestly in every time, it cannot be used as an art except by a republic or a kingdom. And the one and the other of these, when it was well ordered, never consented to any of its citizens or subjects using it as an art, nor did any good man ever practise it as his particular art[. . .]. And I say that Pompey and Caesar, and almost all those captains who were in Rome after the last Carthaginian war, acquired fame as able, not as good, men; those who had lived before them acquired glory as able and good. This arose because these men did not take the practice of war as their art, and those that I named first used it as their art. And while that republic lived immaculately, never did any great citizen presume by means of such a practice to take advantage of the peace by breaking the laws, despoiling the provinces, usurping and tyrannizing the fatherland and taking advantage in every mode. Nor did anyone of obscure fortune think of violating the oath, adhering to private men, not fearing the Senate, or pursuing any tyrannical insult so as to be able to live by the art of war in every time. But those who were captains, contented with their triumph, used to return to private life with desire; and those who were members used to lay down their arms with a greater swiftness than they picked them

up. And everyone used to return to the art by means of which he
had ordered his life; nor was there ever anyone who hoped to be
able to nourish himself with spoils and with this art. [. . .] But
because these good men who do not use war as their art do not
want to draw from it anything but toil, dangers, and glory, when
they are sufficiently glorious they desire to return home and live
from their art. How much it is true of the base men and the
common soldiers that they kept the same orders appears [from
the facts] that each willingly withdrew from such a practice, and
when he was not in the military he wanted not to be in the military, and when he was in the military he would have wanted to be
discharged. This agrees with many modes, especially seeing how
among the first privileges that the Roman people gave to one of
its citizens was that he would not be constrained to soldier
against his will. Therefore while Rome was well ordered (which
was until the Gracchi), it did not have any soldier who took this
practice as an art; yet it had a few wicked ones and these were
severely punished. So a well-ordered city ought to want this study
of war to be used in times of peace for training and in times of
war for necessity and for glory, and the public alone left to use it
as an art, as Rome did. And any citizen who has another end in
such a practice is not good; and any city governed otherwise is
not well ordered.

                                        The Art of War, *I.51–76*

War is for Machiavelli the greatest evil. Through his own direct
experience, and through the reports of Florentine military commanders and commissaries, he knew very well what war is like.
He describes it as a 'pitiable and cruel affection of miserable mor-
tals' that displeases God. In war men unleash their ferocity and
their cruelty, particularly on women, children and non-combatants. When the Spaniards conquered Prato in August 1512, he
writes to an unidentified noblewoman in the September of that
year, 'more than four thousand men were killed and the others
were prisoners and in different ways were forced to ransom

themselves; and they did not spare virgins who were cloistered in the holy places, all of which were filled with rape and sacrilege'.

He describes war as the outcome of ambition, and as a cruel, inhuman, horrible sufferance.[20] Even when a people fights to recover its liberty, war unleashes cruelty. His description of a civil strife in Florentine history conveys a deep sense of revulsion: 'Messer Guglielmo and his son were placed among thousands of their enemies, and the son was not yet eighteen years old; nonetheless, his age, his form, and his innocence could not save him from the fury of the multitude. Those whom they could not wound living, they wounded when dead, and not satisfied with cutting them to pieces with their swords, they tore them apart with their hands and their teeth.' The fact that the perpetrators were Florentines does not prevent Machiavelli from denouncing the episode as a horrible cruelty worthy of the most severe blame (*FH*, II.37).

In spite of its horrors, war is sometimes inevitable, particularly when the survival of a people itself is in danger. This is the case of wars caused by massive migrations, when 'an entire people, with all its families, removes from a place, necessitated by either famine or war, and goes to seek a new seat and a new province, not to command it [. . .] but to posses it all individually' (*D*, II.8). War is also necessary when the price of peace is servitude. In the *Discourses* Machiavelli approvingly repeats the words of the Samnites' political leaders – a brave population settled in the east–central region of Italy that resisted Rome's expansionism for centuries – who explained that 'they had rebelled because peace was harsher for slaves than was war for the free' (*D*, III.44). Last, war may be necessary to expand a territorial mass to secure a republic or kingdom from aggressive neighbours.

Machiavelli affirms in *The Prince* that 'the main foundations of all states are good laws and good armies. Since it is impossible to have good laws if good armies are lacking, and if there are good armies there must also be good laws' (*P*, XII). In *The Art of War* he carries the argument further. Unlike the modern view, which holds that military and civil life are incompatible with one another, the classics rightly teach us that the two are compatible and one requires the other 'because all the arts that are provided for in a civil community for the sake of the common good of men, all the statutes made in it so that men will live in fear of the laws and of God, would be vain if for them there were not provided defences, which when well ordered, preserve them, even though they themselves are not well ordered. And so, on the contrary, good customs, without military support, suffer the same sort of injury as do the rooms of a splendid and kingly palace, even though ornamented with gems and gold, when, not being roofed over, they have nothing to protect them from the rain' (*AW*, Preface).

Good leaders of a republic and princes must not imitate the bad example set by Italian princes of his own times, who believed that a 'prince needed only to think of a sharp reply in his study, to write a fine letter, to show quickness and cleverness in quotable sayings and replies, to know how to spin a fraud, to be adorned with gems and with gold, to sleep and eat with greater splendour than others, to be surrounded with wanton pleasures, to deal with subjects avariciously and proudly, to decay in laziness, to give position in the army by favour, to despise anybody who showed the many praiseworthy course, and to expect their words to be taken as the responses of oracles'. Great political leaders must 'love peace' but 'know how to make war' (*AW*, I.12). They must never rely on mercenary or auxiliary troops (soldiers sent by an allied power under the command of their captains), who 'are disunited, ambitious, undisciplined, and disloyal'. Mercenaries are brave with their friends and cowards with their enemies. They have no fear of God, and they keep no faith with men. They have no other love nor other motive to keep them in the field than a poor salary, which is not enough to make them want to die for the republic or the prince that hires them. They love being soldiers when they are not fighting war, but when war comes, they either flee or desert. It would require little effort, Machiavelli explains, 'to demonstrate, that the ruin of Italy is caused by nothing than its having relied for a period of many years on mercenary troops' (*P*, XII). In the *Discourses* he asserts the same principle in even stronger terms: 'present princes and modern republics that lack their own soldiers for defence and offence ought to be ashamed of themselves' (*D*, I.21).

Attached as he was to the Roman military model, he maintains that 'artillery is useful in an army when ancient virtue is mixed in, but without that, against a virtuous army, it is very useless' (*D*, II.17). He also claims that infantry is more important than horses, that 'fortresses are generally much more harmful than useful', and that 'not gold, as the common opinion cries out, but good soldiers are the sinew of war: for gold is not sufficient to find good soldiers, but good soldiers are quite sufficient to find gold' (*D*, II.10). Following again the Roman example, he believed that military commanders should decide how to conduct the war without discussing every move with political authorities. A great military commander must also speak to the troops, because in war persuasion is often more important than strict discipline. Religious worship too must be held in the greatest respect. Religion and the oath that ancient soldiers were compelled to take, Machiavelli remarks, 'was very valuable' in keeping them well disposed and disciplined, 'for in each of their errors they were menaced not only by those evils that they could fear from men, but by those that they could expect from God' (*AW*, IV.141–3).

Machiavelli wanted soldiers to be exactly the opposite of the soldiers of his own time: loyal to their republic or their king, audacious against the enemy but respectful of the lives and properties of non-combatants: ready to fight for the liberty of their country but eager to see any war end as soon as possible, and, more importantly, restrained by the fear of God that makes oaths effective. The lamentation of Fabrizio Colonna in *The Art of War*

about the soldiers' irreligiousness exemplifies in the best manner
Machiavelli's despair about armies in his own times: 'With what
would I make ashamed those who have been born and raised
without shame? [. . .] By what God, or by what saints would I
make them swear? By those that they adore, or by those that they
curse? I do not know any that they adore, but I know well that
they curse them all. How would I believe that they would
observe their promises to those whom every hour they disparage? How can those who disparage God revere men? What good
form, then, could there be that one could impress on this
matter?' (AW, VII.217–24)

If properly practised, the art of war gives glory. Machiavelli
praises the ethos of pagan religion because it 'beatified only men
full of worldly glory' and blames Christianity because it has been
teaching 'humility, abjection and contempt of the world'. Once
again, Machiavelli wants to restore the ancient view over modern
beliefs and to see men committed to worldly glory over their salvation. He goes as far as to say that a prince who truly seeks
worldly glory should live in a corrupt city, 'not to complete its
corruption, as Caesar did, but to reform it, as Romulus did'.
Worldly glory can be eternal, if it is true. Those who institute
and preserve a republic or a kingdom obtain 'immortal honour';
and death makes the redeemers of republics glorious forever in
this world, as opposed to those who have corrupted a republic
(D, I.10). In The Prince, he assures the new ruler that if he dili-
gently follow Machiavelli's advice, he shall obtain the 'double
glory of founding a new state and of adorning it with good laws,
good armies, good friends, and good examples' (P, XXIV). And
if the same new prince accomplishes the grand deed of liberat-
ing Italy from the barbarians, he will surely attain a glory
comparable to that of Moses, Cyrus and Theseus (P, XXVI).
When Machiavelli addresses members of the Medici family, he
specifies that if they follow his counsel, they will obtain a glory
greater than that of their ancestors: 'Among so much good fortune that God has bestowed on your family and Your Holiness

personally, this is the greatest, namely, the power and the material to make yourself immortal, and thus greatly surpass the glory of your father and ancestors.'[21]

However heaven or God contribute to it, glory is a worldly reward; one way of living eternally in this world is by remaining alive in the memory of humanity. The other path is eternal disgrace, a destiny which ought to be as frightening as the other is appealing. Like virtues and vices, the path of glory and that of infamy are very close. It is easy to mistake the former for the latter. Machiavelli's advice is never to become a tyrant. Tyranny makes princes and kings lose 'glory, security, tranquillity, and peace of mind', and brings instead 'infamy, scorn, abhorrence, danger and disquiet'. Since they destroy republics and kingdoms and are enemies of virtue, tyrants are the most infamous and detestable of all men. And yet, in spite of the dangers and the infamy, many men have become tyrants, and many more would have done so had they not been stopped. They err either voluntarily or by mere ignorance; in both cases, however, the cause of their error is deceit, and what they are deceived by is 'a false good and a false glory' (D, I.10), like the Florentines, who long 'not for true glory, but for the contemptible honours on which hatreds, enmities, differences, and sects depend' (FH, III.59).

To this sort of false glory – which has caused humanity innumerable sufferances – belongs Caesar's glory. In spite of the lauds of historians and writers, no one 'should be deceived by Caesar's renown ["gloria"]', Machiavelli admonishes (D, I.10). By Machiavelli's standards, military prowess and the ability to preserve one's power are not sufficient. The infamous Agatocles was an excellent captain of great virtue who confronted and survived dangers and displayed an 'indomitable spirit' in enduring and overcoming adversities. By killing his fellow-citizens, betraying his friends, being treacherous, merciless and irreligious, Agatocles gained and maintained power, but 'not glory'; and, Machiavelli specifies, he does not deserve to be ranked 'among the finest men' (P, VIII). To attain glory one has to be valiant and good, like the Roman generals before the last Punic War who 'gained glory as brave and good', whereas the captains like Caesar and Pompey acquired only fame as brave men (*AW*). In spite of their outstanding qualities, they missed the path of glory because ambition perverted their judgement and drove them to break laws, plunder provinces, tyrannize their country and gain wealth for themselves. As he remarks in the *Discourses*, love of true glory is a frein which drives men to be good (*D*, II.33).

Machiavelli then fully endorses the classical view that there is a clear distinction between fame and glory.[22] Fame is the reward for military or political deeds which are in one way or another grand, noteworthy or extraordinary, and thereby give a lasting or even an eternal reputation and renown. Had the tyrant of Perugia, Giovanpagolo Baglioni, had the courage to kill his arch-enemy Pope Julius II when he imprudently arrived in the city accompanied only by the cardinals and a few soldiers, he would have gained 'an immortal fame' but would not have attained glory. He would have gained a lasting reputation because he would have been the first 'to show prelates how little men are respected who live and rule as they do, and would have done a thing the greatness of which would have obliterated any infamy and any danger that might arise from it'. But the wickedness of that action, and his incestuous deeds, barred him from the path to true glory (*D*, I.27).

Machiavelli acknowledges that in some cases men's judgement is less severe than his own. Common people are impressed by 'appearances and results' (*P*, XVIII). They equate fame with glory, as in the case of King Ferdinand of Aragon who had become 'in fame and glory' the 'first king of the Christendom' (*P*, XXI). He achieved this status in a very short time because, Machiavelli explains, he performed great enterprises and extraordinary deeds. In an earlier chapter of *The Prince*, Machiavelli remarks that had Ferdinand of Aragon been trustworthy, he 'would have lost either reputation or power several times over' (*P*, XVIII). However, Machiavelli attributes King Ferdinand reputation but not glory: 'I will say but this, I do not mean that a fraud which involves breaking your word or the contracts you have made is glorious; for, although on occasion it may win a state or a kingdom, it will never bring you glory' (*D*, III.40).

Machiavelli maintains that glory, along with riches, is one of the ends 'which everyone aims at'. His objective was to rekindle the love of glory and direct it toward its proper goals. He puts before his contemporaries' eyes the grand deeds of princes, captains and lawgivers who founded or reformed republics and kingdoms. He also describes the example of the Roman people, which had been for four hundred years a 'lover of glory and of the common good of its country' (*D*, I.58), as well as the example of eminent compatriots, like Lorenzo il Magnifico, who upon his return from a dangerous diplomatic mission was received as a 'very great man' (*FH*, VIII.19).

At the same time, Machiavelli expresses contempt for princes insensitive to the allure of glory, like the 'lesser princes' of Italy, who were 'unmoved by any glory' and only sought 'to live either more rich or more secure' (*FH*, I.39). He saw the love of glory as the only motive for the grand deeds that liberty at times demands, like resisting tyranny and mobilizing citizens against arrogant men who want to impose their domination.

7

THE NECESSITY OF RELIGION

Thinking then whence it can arise that in those ancient times people were more lovers of freedom than in these, I believe it arises from the same cause that makes men less strong now, which I believe is the difference between our education and the ancient, founded on the difference between our religion and the ancient. For our religion, having shown the truth and the true way, makes us esteem less the honour of the worlds, whereas the Gentiles, esteeming it very much and having placed the highest good in it, were more ferocious in their actions. This can be inferred from many of their institutions, beginning from the magnificence of their sacrifices as against the humility of ours, where there is some pomp more delicate than magnificent but no ferocious or vigorous action. Neither pomp nor magnificence of ceremony was lacking there, but the action of the sacrifice, full of blood and ferocity, was added, with a multitude of animals being killed there. This sight, being terrible, rendered men similar to itself. Besides this, the ancient religion did not beatify men if they were not fully of worldly glory, as were captains of armies and princes of republics. Our religion has glorified humble and contemplative more than active men. It has placed the highest good in humility, abjectness, and contempt of things human; the other placed it in greatness of spirit, strength of body, and in all other things capable of making men very strong.

And if our religion asks that you have strength in yourself, it wishes you to be capable more of suffering than of doing something strong. This mode of life thus seems to have rendered the world weak and given it in prey to criminal men, who can manage it securely, seeing that the collectivity of men, so as to go to paradise, think more of enduring their beatings than of avenging them. And although the world appears to be made effeminate and heaven disarmed it arises without doubt more from the cowardice of the men who have interpreted our religion according to idleness and not according to virtue. For if they considered how it permits us the exaltation and defence of the fatherland, they would see that it wishes us to love and honour it and to prepare ourselves to be such that we can defend it. These educations and false interpretations thus bring it about that not as many republics are seen in the world as were seen in antiquity; nor, as a consequence, is as much love of freedom seen in peoples as was then.

Discourses on Livy, *II.2*

Machiavelli was a severe critic of Christianity. Not only did he ridicule monks, friars, priests and popes with devastating irony, but he believed the papal court of Rome responsible for Italy's political disunion and decay. 'Because of the wicked examples of that court,' he writes, 'this province has lost all devotion and all religion – which brings with it infinite inconveniences and infinite disorders; for as where there is religion one presupposes every good, so where it is missing one presupposes the contrary. Thus we have this first obligation to the Church and to the priest that we have become without religion and wicked.' Machiavelli goes as far as to write that if the court of Rome were to move to Switzerland, where there are 'the only peoples who live according to the ancients as regards both religion and military orders', in a few years they would corrupt even those most virtuous citizens.

In addition Machiavelli writes that the Church of Rome, for

fear of losing its political power and wealth, has always success-
fully prevented the political unification of Italy: 'the Church has
kept and keeps this province divided. And truly no province has
ever been united or happy unless it has all come under obedience
to one republic or to one prince, as happened to France or
Spain. The cause that Italy is not in the same condition and does
not also have one republic or one prince to govern it is solely the
Church' (D, I.12). Even more devastating is the accusation that
Machiavelli launches against Catholic religion in the passage that
opens this chapter. He declares that Catholic religion has rendered the world weak and destroyed the love of liberty that was
so strong in ancient times. Not only has it made the world an
easy prey for wicked men, but it has also deprived peoples, especially the Italians, of the moral resources necessary to resurrect
themselves from servitude.

When he speaks of pagan religion, particularly that of the
ancient Romans, Machiavelli has a completely different view. He
asserts that 'where there is religion one presupposes every good',
whereas 'where it is missing one presupposes the contrary'. He
even puts the 'heads and orderers of religions' above the founders
of kingdoms or republics in the hierarchy of the men who
deserve praise. In his judgement, the Romans owed their glory
more to Numa, who instituted religious worship, than to
Romulus, the founder of political and military institutions: 'for
where there is religion, arms can easily be introduced, and where
there are arms and not religion, the latter can be introduced only
with difficulty'. Without religion the soldiers' oath is meaning-
less, and therefore they cannot be expected to be prepared to
sacrifice their lives defending their country, whereas the fear of
God 'made easier whatever enterprise the Senate or the great
men of Rome might plan to make' (D, I.11).

In times of political and military crisis, religion was a precious
source of moral strength in ancient Rome, even stronger
than the Romans' intense love of country. Machiavelli recounts
the episode of Scipio who, after the tremendous defeat of the

Roman armies at Cannae against Hannibal (216 BC), forced with the sword a number of fellow Roman citizens to take the oath not to abandon Rome, as they were about to do. Those citizens resolved at the end to remain in Rome and defend it because they feared 'to break an oath more than the laws', and 'esteemed the power of God more than the power of men' (*D*, I.11). In his comment Machiavelli magnifies the power of religion, whereas his source, Livy, stresses the courage of Scipio and the fear that he, not God, was able to instil in the hearts of his fellow citizens.

The religion of the Romans 'animated the plebs', stirring them against the arrogance of the Senate, and keeping Rome free from tyranny and corruption. In addition, Roman religion kept 'men good' and brought 'shame to the wicked'. Machiavelli believed that without good mores, civil laws will not make human beings good and that only religion has the power to shape these mores. Religion instils in men's hearts shame in the proper sense, the inward sufferance that comes from the conscience that we have violated the moral law. He also asserts the apparently bizarre idea that religion is more necessary in republics than in principalities because 'where the fear of God fails' one needs 'the fear of the prince which supplies the defects of religion' (*D*, I.11). Religion is a necessary condition for republican liberty, whereas the lack of religion makes peoples apt to serve. The best evidence for this belief is history: all free peoples of antiquity, like the Samnites, the Etruscans and the Romans, were religious; so were the Germans of the free cities, the only free peoples of Machiavelli's times. It matters little to him that the ancient free peoples were pagans and modern ones Christian. He is not interested in the content of their theology. What really matters for him is the kind of civic ethos that religions prescribe and teach. Irreligious peoples, like the Italians of his times, were the most enslaved: politically because they were dominated by kings, tyrants and foreign powers; morally because they had lost their inward strength.

Religion is also necessary for the foundation of new orders, the political task that Machiavelli regarded as the most glorious political achievement. As I have noted, Machiavelli in *The Prince* assures a future redeemer of Italy the help of God. In the *Discourses* he stresses that 'truly there was never any orderer of extraordinary laws for a people who did not have recourse to God, because otherwise they would not have been accepted'. Great lawgivers like Lycurgus, Solon and many others pretended to be inspired by God because their rational arguments in favour of the new laws would not have been sufficient to persuade their fellow citizens. Similarly, in 1494, Girolamo Savonarola invoked God when he encouraged the Florentine elite to institute the Republic that employed Machiavelli as Secretary: 'to the people of Florence it does not appear that they are either ignorant or coarse; nonetheless, they were persuaded by Friar Girolamo Savonarola that he spoke with God. I do not wish to judge whether it is true or not, because one should speak with reverence of such a man; but I do say that an infinite number believed him. For his life, learning, and the subject he took up were sufficient to make them lend faith' (*D*, I.11).

For Machiavelli, religion is essential to found, preserve, and reform political orders and especially republics. Yet he considered the prevalent religion of his times utterly corrupt and corrupting: not a means to attain political liberty, but a powerful obstacle against it. To resolve this contradiction, Machiavelli envisaged several solutions. His first and general piece of advice to princes and leaders of republics is to 'maintain the foundations of the religion they hold', and favour and magnify all things that arise in its favour, even if 'they judge them false'. In this way they will keep their polity religious and in consequence 'good and united' (*D*, I.12). At the same time, he looks for a religion that instils love of liberty and a properly civic ethos.

Some scholars have argued that Machiavelli was dreaming of resurrecting dead pagan religion. In the *Discourses* he seems to say that had the civic aspects of pagan religion been preserved by 'the princes of the Christian republic as was ordered by its giver [Christ]', Christian states 'would be more united, much happier than they are'. However, he knew perfectly well that ancient pagan religion could never be resurrected because Christians 'suppressed all its orders and all its ceremonies and eliminated every memory of that ancient theology' (D, II.5). He did not fantasize about the return to paganism because he believed that Christianity had all the components of a religion of liberty. The tradition of republican Christianity in Florence was based on the principle that a true Christian must be a good citizen who serves the common good in order to implement the divine plan on earth. God participates in human history, loves free republics, supports and rewards those who govern justly, has created men in his own image, and wishes them to become like him with their virtue, working to make the earthly city comparable to the heavenly one. Christ and Cicero, the Apostles and the republican heroes of Rome coexisted for the Florentines, side by side. For the Florentines of Machiavelli's time the true saints were not those ascetics who renounced the world, nor were they devout men and women who obeyed the commandments of the Church; they were the citizens who placed liberty and homeland before all other things.

This interpretation of Christianity was a radical response to the corruption of the Catholic Church, and it called for a religious and moral reformation capable of triggering a rebirth of charity and justice. For Machiavelli the Church of Rome had misinterpreted Christianity; it interpreted Christianity according to idleness and not, as it should be, 'according to virtue': 'For if they considered how it [Christianity] permits us the exaltation and defence of the fatherland, they would see that it wishes us to love and honour it and to prepare ourselves to be such that we can defend it' (D, II.2). Properly understood, therefore, Christianity could be that civic religion, the necessary precondition for the resurrection of republican liberty.

Luther launched the Protestant Reformation while Machiavelli was writing his *Discourses on Livy*. In this work

Machiavelli envisaged a religious and moral reformation designed to educate free citizens. He had in mind the resurrection of the founding principles of republics and of Christianity. Justice must be rediscovered, both to punish those men who violate constitutional laws, no matter how powerful, and to reward the most virtuous citizens who have properly served the common good. He also urges the restoration of proper religious worship. The process through which a republic turns to its founding principles is described as re-examination: 'It is thus necessary, as was said, that men who live together in any order whatever often examine themselves either through these extrinsic accidents or through intrinsic ones' (D, III.1). He cites Saint Francis and Saint Dominic, who lived according to Christian poverty and imitated 'the example of the life of Christ' at the end of the seventeenth century as a possible model for reform. But their reform did not bring about a general reformation of the Church because they taught that 'it is evil to say evil of evil, and that it is good to live under obedience to them [the corrupt prelates] and if they make an error, to leave them for God to punish'. Nonetheless, they brought back into the minds of people of Christian faith the original tenets of Christianity.

The kind of reformation for which Machiavelli was hoping had both a political and a religious character: a rediscovery of justice and love of country, and a rediscovery of the Christian practice of charity. His hopes were frustrated. Instead of a political reform that would have resuscitated political liberty, political oppression eroded the fibres of Italy; instead of a religious reform, Italy went through a religious counterreformation, which established a religiosity that strengthened a servile mentality, sustaining centuries of political oppression. In contrast, those countries where the Reformation took hold, like England, Holland and above all the United States of America, were able to conquer and defend political liberty. Of all Machiavelli's great intuitions, that of the connection between political liberty and religion has proven to be the most wise.

8

A PHILOSOPHER OF LIBERTY

Cities, and especially those not well ordered that are administered under the name of republic, frequently change their governments and their states not between liberty and servitude, as many believe, but between servitude and license. For only the name of freedom is extolled by the ministers of license, who are the men of the people, and by the ministers of servitude, who are the nobles, neither of them desiring to be subject either to the laws or to men. True, when it happens (and it happens rarely) that by the good fortune of a city there rises in it a wise, good, and powerful citizen by whom laws are ordered by which these humours of the nobles and the men of the people are quieted or restrained so that they cannot do evil, then that city can be called free and that state be judged stable and firm: for a city based on good laws and good orders has no necessity, as have others, for the virtue of a single man to maintain it. Many ancient republics endowed with such laws and orders had states with long lives; all those republics that have lacked and are lacking such orders and laws have frequently changed and are changing their governments from a tyrannical to a licentious state, and back again. In these, through the powerful enemies each of them has, there neither is nor can be any stability, because one state displeases good men, the other displeases the wise; the one can do evil easily, the other can do good only with difficulty; in the one the insolent men

have too much authority, in the other [the] fools. And both the
one and the other must be maintained by the virtue and the fortune of a single man who can either fail by death or become
useless because of this travail.

Florentine Histories, *IV.1*

Even if over the centuries Machiavelli has become famous, or
infamous, as the author of *The Prince*, a work composed to teach
a prince how to found a principality, he was a convinced sup-
porter of republican liberty, and he wrote the most eloquent and
convincing arguments in its defence, above all in the *Discourses on
Livy*. One may ask how the same person can be a republican and
write *The Prince*. Of the many interpretations that scholars
have advanced over the centuries, the most correct is the one
that Machiavelli himself suggests in his letter to Vettori of 10
December 1513. He says that he intended to prove that he knew
better than anybody else what it takes to found and preserve a
principality that can guarantee legality and order, and accomplish
great things like the unification of Italy, or at least a large part of
it. He was also hoping that the Medici, in recognition of his
competence and the integrity that he had displayed during his
fifteen years' service to the republic, would offer him a post in
Florence or Rome (where Giovanni de' Medici was pope under
the name of Leo X). Even if the Medici regime had almost
entirely dismantled the Republican government for which
Machiavelli had worked, serving in office was still the only way
to do good for Florence, for Italy and for himself. Politics – real
political engagement – was his deepest vocation. Life outside
politics was for him empty, even if he managed to adapt to it. For
this reason, as a republican living in a time of principalities, he
composed *The Prince*.

Liberty is for Machiavelli the highest and most precious political value. In full agreement with classical republican political
theory, and with Florentine republicans in the Quattrocento, he
understood political liberty as absence of domination. Individuals

are free, in his view, when they are not dependent on a tyrant or an oligarchy that imposes its arbitrary will. The same definition applies to cities and peoples: a city or a people are free as long as they are independent of the will of other cities or peoples. Cities, Machiavelli explains at the outset of the *Discourses*, have been founded either by 'free men' or by men 'depending on others' (*D*, I.1). In the second case, Machiavelli adds, their accomplishments are rarely comparable to those of free cities like Rome.

He also stressed many times that political liberty can be enjoyed only under a republican government. 'All the states,' he writes, 'all the dominions that have held sway over men, have been either republics or principalities'; a few lines later he equates a republic with being free: 'used to living under a prince or used to being free'. When cities or countries live under a prince the inhabitants are used to obeying and they do not know how to embrace a free way of life. In the chapter of *The Prince* on civil principality, he mentions three mutually exclusive possibilities: a principality, a republic or a license. In the *Discourses* he asserts that 'he who sets out to govern a multitude' can do so either 'through freedom' or 'through a principality' (*D*, I.16). In another chapter he remarks that in ancient times the peoples of Italy 'were all of them free', and among them 'one never hears of there being any kings' (*D*, II.2). Discussing the Italian towns subject to Venice's dominion, he remarks that since 'they are accustomed to live under a prince, and not free, they are accustomed to serve' (*D*, III.12).

For Machiavelli political liberty is incompatible with monarchical or princely government because subjects are precluded from participation in sovereign deliberations and the appointment of magistrates. They may enjoy a modicum of security, but this is always precarious because of their dependency on the monarch's will, and they have no power over laws that serve his own or others' particular interest. They can be oppressed at any moment, and this constant possibility inevitably generates feelings of fear, which in turn stimulate servile habits utterly incompatible with the status and the duties of a free people. The absence of fear and servility are the distinctive features of a truly free people. 'The common interest that results from republican self government' is 'not fearing for the honour of wives and that of children, not to be afraid for oneself' (D, I.16). As long as 'the republic lasted incorrupt', Machievelli states, the Roman people 'never served humbly' (D, I.58).

Republics are more apt to grant political liberty to citizens because they are better disposed to carry out actions for the common good. Citizens of republics are 'more prudent, more stable, and of better judgement than a prince, for one sees a universal opinion produce marvellous effects in its forecast, so that it appears to foresee its ill and its good by a hidden virtue' (D, I.58). Once they have identified their common good, republican governments have the power to enforce it: 'And without doubt this common good is not observed if not in republics, since all that is for that purpose is executed, and although it may turn out to arm this or that private individual, those for whom the aforesaid does good are so many that they can go ahead with it against the disposition of the few crushed by it' (D, II.2).

Even if sovereign power – the power of passing laws and appointing representatives and magistrates – belongs in a republic to the people, it must always be exercised under the statutes and the laws. Both princes and republics 'have had need of being regulated by the laws. For a prince who can do what he wishes is crazy; a people that can do what it wishes is not wise' (D, I.58). In addition to the restraint of laws, popular power must be checked by other types of power that Machiavelli calls regal and aristocratic. Following once again classical republican tradition, he maintains that to protect the common good and the rule of law, a well-ordered republic must have a mixed government, like Sparta, where Lycurgus 'ordered his laws as to give their roles to the kings, the aristocrats, and the people and made a state that lasted more than eight hundred years, achieving the highest praise for himself and quiet in that city', or Rome, which became a 'perfect republic' when, with the establishment of the tribunes of the plebs, it became a mixed republic with a kingly element in the consuls, an aristocratic element in the Senate, a popular element in the assembly (*D*, I.2). Of the three elements that compose a good republican government, however, the popular one must have a greater weight over the other two and be the real guardian of liberty: 'I say that one should put on guard over a thing those who have less appetite for usurping it. Without doubt, if one considers the end of the nobles and of the ignobles, one will see a great desire to dominate in the former, and in the latter only desire not to be dominated; and in consequence, a greater will to live free, being less able to usurp it than are the great' (*D*, I.5).

To properly ensure liberty, the first and constant preoccupation of a good republic must be to protect the laws. In the *Discourses*, Machiavelli contrasts political life with tyranny understood as authority unbound by laws, and opposes armed violence to 'civil modes and customs' (*D*, I.25, I.37). In the *Florentine Histories* he again contrasts civil life with 'sole authority' (*FH*, VIII.1). When he speaks of rule of law, Machiavelli means the observance of a legality where men's actions are judged by general rules which apply equally to all. Like the jurists, he sees the generality and the impartiality of the law as the foundation of civil life and liberty. The laws, he says, 'make [men] good' – that is, compel them to serve the common good and refrain from harming their fellow citizens, as civil and political life demands (*D*, I.3).

A wise legislator must frame the laws assuming that 'all men are wicked', and that they will always behave with malignity, if they have the opportunity. As he has written many times, and with particular emphasis in *The Prince* (XVII), men are 'ungrateful, fickle, simulators and deceivers, avoiders of danger, and greedy for gain'. They forget 'the death of their father more quickly than the loss of their patrimony'. The law is therefore necessary, and once it is in place, it must be obeyed without permitting privilege or discrimination. Crimes have to be punished regardless of the personal and public merits of the criminal. No well-ordered republic, he writes, 'allows the demerits of its citizens to be cancelled out by their merits; but having prescribed rewards for a good deed and punishments for a bad one and having rewarded someone for doing well, if the same person afterward does wrong, it punishes him, regardless of any of the good deeds he has done'. Should this principle of legal justice be disregarded, he concludes, 'civil life will soon disappear' (D, I.24).

Machiavelli strongly advises that to remain well ordered, and to prevent corruption, a republic must inflict punishments according to the law and only by legitimate public authorities, never by private citizens acting outside the law. Coriolanus, a Roman nobleman who ordered that corn be held back from the plebs to diminish their political power, was saved from popular fury by the tribunes who summoned him to appear in court. Had the mob lynched him, Machiavelli remarks, his death would have been a wrong inflicted by private citizens on a private citizen. This violation of legality would have caused mistrust in the efficacy of the law to provide adequate protection. Citizens would have formed factions to protect themselves, leading to the downfall of the republic. But since the matter was settled by public authorities in full respect of the law, in an orderly way, the Roman republic did not suffer serious consequences (D, I.7).

Rule of law also means laws and statutes that aim at the common good. As a citizen eloquently explains in the *Histories*, to restore a 'free and civil life' Florence needs new laws and statutes to protect the common good, and to replace the rule of factions that has imposed 'orders and laws made not for the public but for personal utility, not in accordance with free life but by the ambition of that party which is in power' (*FH*, III.5). When the Roman republic became corrupt, 'only the powerful proposed laws, not for the common liberty, but to augment their own power' (D, I.18).

A republic must protect freedom of speech with the greatest diligence and determination, especially in sovereign councils. Machiavelli refers to the ancient Roman republic where 'a tribune or any other citizen could propose to the people a law, in regard to which every citizen was entitled to speak either in favour of it or against it, prior to a decision being reached'. It is a good thing, Machiavelli comments, 'that everyone should be at liberty to express his opinion', so that 'when the people have heard what each has to say they may choose the best plan' (*D*, I.18). Unlike other republican theorists, before him and after him, he did not fear the corrupting power of eloquence. He trusted the citizens' good judgement: 'if a people hears two orators who incline to different sides, when they are of equal virtue [ability], very few times does one see it not take up the better opinion, and not persuaded of the truth that it hears' (*D*, I.58). However, with his typical wisdom, he also recognized that 'many times, deceived by a false image of good, the people desires its own ruin; and if it is not made aware what is bad and what the good, by someone in whom it has faith, infinite dangers and harms are brought into republics. When fate makes the people not have faith in someone, as happens at some time after it has been deceived in the past either by things or by men, it of necessity comes to ruin' (*D*, I.53).

True political liberty cannot tolerate exclusions and discriminations and must instead reward only virtue. In a republic, citizens are confident that their children 'will have the chance to become rulers', if they are virtuous; in a principality, on the contrary, this chance is precluded, because the prince 'cannot bestow honours on the valiant and good citizens, since he does not want to have any cause to suspect them' (*D*, II.2). A republic rewards citizens 'only for honest and determined reasons, and apart from this rewards and honours no one' (*D*, I.16). A prince, on the contrary, can be easily persuaded to bestow public honours upon corrupt men (*D*, I.58). Finally, and this is for Machiavelli a consideration of the greatest importance, in a good republic poor citizens have the same chance to attain public honours as anybody else: in Rome 'poverty did not bar you from any office or from any honour, and virtue was sought out no matter in whose house it dwelt' (*D*, III.25). If the citizens appoint the magistrates, there are better chances that the positions of highest responsibility and prestige are filled by the most eminent citizens. This is yet another reason why a republican government is the most fit to preserve a true political order. It is in fact against the basic principle of any good political order not to appoint grave and honoured citizens to the highest offices of the state.

Machiavelli's belief that republics are better than monarchies and principalities because they entrust political power to the best citizens was, and still is, a hope rather than a reality. In effect citizens of republics are often morally corrupt or utterly unwise and they are the easy dupes of demagogues. As a result they often appoint incompetent or corrupt people. Machiavelli was perfectly aware of the malignant effects of political corruption in republics, and yet he continued to believe that republics are better than monarchies because, after all, they are more able to ensure the highest good of political liberty under the shield of law.

9

SOCIAL CONFLICTS AND POLITICAL ORDER

I say that to me it appears that those who damn the tumults between the nobles and the plebs blame those things that were the first cause of keeping Rome free, and that they consider the noises and the cries that would arise in such tumults more than the good effects that they engendered. They do not consider that in every republic are two diverse humours, that of the people and that of the great, and that all the laws that are made in favour of freedom arise from their disunion, as can easily be seen to have occurred in Rome. For from the Tarquins to the Gracchi, which was more than three hundred years, the tumults of Rome rarely engendered exile and very rarely blood. Neither can these tumults, therefore, be judged harmful nor a republic divided that in so much time sent no more than eight or ten citizens into exile because of its differences, and killed very few of them, and condemned not many more to fines of money. Nor can one in any mode, with reason, call a republic disordered where there are so many examples of virtue; for good examples arise from good education, good education from good laws, and good laws from those tumults that many inconsiderately damn. For whoever examines their end well will find that they have engendered not any exile or violence unfavourable to the common good but laws and orders in benefit of public freedom. If anyone said the modes were extraordinary and almost wild, to see the people together crying out against the Senate, the Senate against the people, running tumultuously through the streets, closing shops, the whole plebs leaving Rome – all of which things frighten whoever does no other than read them – I say that every city ought to have its modes with which the people can vent its ambition, and especially those cities that wish to avail themselves of the people in important things. Among these the city of Rome had this mode: that when the people wished to obtain a law, either they did one of those things said above or they refused to enrol their names to go to war, so that to placate them there was need to satisfy them in some part. The desires of free peoples are rarely pernicious to freedom because they arise either from being oppressed or from suspicion that they may be oppressed. If these opinions are false, there is for them the remedy of assemblies, where some good man gets up who in orating demonstrates to them how they deceive themselves: and though peoples, as Tully says, are ignorant, they are capable of truth and easily yield when the truth is told them by a man worthy of faith.

Discourses on Livy, *I.4*

Machiavelli is the first political theorist to maintain that social conflicts are a powerful means to protect political liberty, if they do not degenerate into armed confrontations and remain within the limits of civil life. He was not, however, a populist who unconditionally praised the people's hostility towards the nobility. He also bitterly reproaches the ambition of the populace. Not content with having secured their position in regard to the nobles, he remarks, the Roman plebs began to quarrel with the nobles out of ambition and to demand a share also in the distribution of honours and of property. This, he concludes, grew into a disease, which led to the dispute over the Agrarian Law and in the end caused the destruction of the republic (*D*, I.37). The ambition of the nobility would have ruined Rome's liberty much earlier, had not the plebs kept them in check for three hundred years. In several cases, however, it was necessary to restrain the tribunes of the plebs too, because their ambition was harmful to the common good and the safety of the fatherland (*D*, III.11).

Even more eloquent than Rome was the example of Florence, where the people wanted to completely exclude the nobility from government. Whereas the desire of the Roman people to share with the nobles the highest honours was reasonable, that of the people of Florence was 'injurious and unjust'. With their exaggerated requests, the people of Florence pushed the nobility to armed violence. Moreover, as long as the people of Florence shared the highest posts in the government with the nobles, they acquired 'the same virtue' that was typical of the nobility. But when they excluded the nobility from government, Florence could no longer avail itself of that 'virtue in arms and the generosity of spirit that were in the nobility', and became more and more 'humble and abject' (*FH*, III.1). In ancient Rome, on the contrary, social conflicts between the plebs and the nobles led to laws and statutes that satisfied, at least to some extent, the plebs' and the nobles' interests and therefore helped to preserve political liberty. From the study of this historical experience Machiavelli derives a general piece of advice for modern republics – namely, that 'in every republic there are two humours, that of the populace and that of the nobility and that all legislation favourable to liberty is brought about by the clash between them' (*D*, I.4).

His praise of social conflict is consistent with his commitment to the principles of civil life. When he stresses the good effects of social conflicts, he refers to conflicts that were settled 'by disputing', as in Rome, not 'by fighting', as in Florence (*FH*, III.1). He also promoted a political principle that became one of the main tenets of later democratic thought – namely, that people's desires are rarely if at all pernicious to liberty. 'If we consider the goals of the nobility and of the common people,' he argues, 'it will be clear that the nobility desires to dominate, whereas the ordinary people only desire not to be dominated and consequently to live free.' It is therefore reasonable to believe that the ordinary people will take greater care to protect liberty: 'since it is impossible for them to usurp power, they will not permit others to do so'. He knows that advocates of aristocratic governments claim it is safer to give a predominant role to the nobility – to satisfy their ambitions – while the plebs, stripped of political power, do not cause endless trouble in the republic, as the examples of ancient Sparta and Venice amply prove. To rebut this he remarks that the nobles are much more dangerous than the ordinary citizens because they are afraid of losing what they possess, and have more means than the people to alter the constitution. Everything considered, Machiavelli concludes, it is wiser to trust ordinary citizens, and not to fear their claims, if one wants to establish and preserve a truly civil and free way of living (D, I.5).

A republic, then, is well ordered only when each component of the city has its proper place. Machiavelli cites Sparta, where Lycurgus introduced a constitution that 'assigned to the kings, to the aristocracy, and to the populace each its own function, and thus introduced a form of government which lasted for more than eight hundred years to his very great credit and to the tranquillity of that city', and Rome, which became a perfect republic when, after the tribunes were instated, 'all three estates had now a share' in the government (D, I.3). As an example of a badly ordered republic Machiavelli points to Florence, which never had a constitution capable of recognizing each social group and therefore oscillated between governments that were either too popular or too aristocratic.

Machiavelli stresses that a well-instituted republic must encourage the citizens' participation by rewarding civic virtue, and entrust the highest public posts to citizens who have displayed outstanding talents in serving the common good. For him citizens who have shown themselves suitable should be allowed to ascend into public office, and those whose lives do not render them worthy should not be appointed to government posts. A good political and civil order must therefore have a hierarchy of honour based upon virtue; that is, it must be just. In a republic, Machiavelli writes in the *Discourses*, citizens are confident that their children 'will have the chance to become rulers' if they are virtuous; in a principality, this chance is precluded, because the prince 'cannot bestow honours on the valiant and good citizens, since he does not want to have any cause to suspect them' (*D*, II.2). Moreover, a republic rewards citizens 'only for honest and determined reasons, and apart from this rewards and honours no one' (*D*, I.16). A prince, on the contrary, can be easily persuaded to bestow public honours upon corrupt men (*D*, I.58). Finally, and for Machiavelli this is a consideration of the greatest importance, in a good republic poor citizens have the same chance to attain public honours as anybody else: in Rome 'poverty did not bar you from any office or from any honour, and virtue was sought out no matter in whose house it dwelt' (*D*, III). If the citizens appoint the magistrates there is a better chance that the highest positions of responsibility and prestige will be filled by the most eminent citizens. As Machiavelli writes in a text on the 1521 constitutional reform of Florence, it is against any political order not to appoint grave and honoured citizens to the highest offices of the republic.[23]

A well-ordered republic, according to Machiavelli, does not need to be quiet. The Venetians should rather renounce their social peace if its cost is a constitution that does not protect its own independence (*D*, I.6). Venice, Machiavelli remarks, was able to preserve its much-vaunted social peace by restricting the number of citizens with full political rights and by not employing those without full rights in war. This constitutional arrangement was good as long as the city was powerful enough to discourage potential aggressors and was able to remain free without expansion. But a city may need to expand its territory to weaken a powerful and aggressive neighbour. In this case, a constitution designed to preserve social peace turns out to be an obstacle to the city's liberty. Machiavelli urges his readers to abandon this model of the 'true political life and true quiet of a city' and tries to persuade them that even a tumultuous republic with a large population and a civic army can have a fully civil life, if it respects the principles of the rule of law and the common good, with the additional advantage of being more secure and more honourable (*D*, I.6).

Machiavelli was not an admirer of conquest, as it has been claimed, even if expansion was for him of central importance. Like earlier theorists of communal self-government, he identifies civic greatness with political liberty, urban splendour and territorial expansion. However, territorial aggrandizement does not mean for him predatory expansionism. The ancient Tuscans attained a remarkable greatness not through conquest, but by forming a league of several republics in which no one of them had preference, authority or rank above the others, and 'when other cities were acquired, they made them constituent members in the same way the Swiss act in our times, and as in Greece the Acheans and the Aetolians acted in old times' (*D*, II.4). He praises their foreign politics, which resulted in remarkable glory and sustained laudable customs and religiosity across its empire. He warmly recommends it to his fellow Florentines as being the best model to follow if the imitation of the Romans should appear 'difficult'. At the same time, and not just in the *Discourses* but in all his writings on this subject, he condemns the policy of expansion through conquest and subjection as being 'completely useless' in general, and 'most useless' for unarmed republics.

Even the Roman method of expansion, which he ranks as the best of all, is not predatory, at least not in the way Machiavelli understood it, since it consisted of forming alliances 'in which you reserve yourself the headship, the seat in which the central authority resides, and the right of initiative' and in granting Roman citizenship to conquered and allied peoples. One of the aspects of Roman expansionist policy which he exalts in the most eloquent manner was their practice of letting 'those towns they did not demolish live under their own laws, even those that surrendered not as partners but as subjects' and of not leaving in them 'any sign of the empire of the Roman people but obliged them to some conditions, which, if observed, kept them in their state and dignity'. With equal eloquence he praises the Florentines' protective and benevolent policy toward Pistoia and condemns their predatory policy toward Pisa, Siena and Lucca. The result of the former policy was that 'the Pistoiese run willingly under [the Florentines' rule]'; the result of the latter was that 'the others have exerted and exert all their force so as not to come under it'. His exhortation to employ armed violence only as a last instance 'does not mean I judge that arms and force do not have to be put to work, but they should be reserved for the last place, where and when other modes are not enough' (*D*, II.21).

For Machiavelli the lust for conquest to increase one's own power is not a virtue, but a nefarious vice: it does not lead to greatness, but to ruin. The most frequent cause of the fall of kingdoms and republics, he writes in *The Golden Ass*, is that the powerful 'are never satisfied' with their power. The desire for conquering 'destroys the states', and even if all recognize the error 'none flees from it'. A few lines later, he contrasts Venice, Sparta and Athens, which fell into ruin after they conquered the powers round them, with the German free cities which live 'secure' even if their dominion does not extend more than six miles round about (*OW*, II.762). When he urges the Florentines to provide themselves with good armies, he does not evoke prospects of conquest and predation, and nor does he declare the commonplace of Florence's superiority and its claim over other peoples. On the contrary, he stresses that the Republic needs an army to protect its own liberty. In his oration of 1503, written to persuade the Great Council to authorize new taxes to levy an army against the threat posed by Caesar Borgia, he states that no wise king or republic has ever put its state at the mercy of other powers or has considered itself to be secure when it had to count on others' help. He offers on this matter a precise rule: 'each city, each state must regard as enemies all those powers which can occupy its territory and against which it cannot defend itself'.[24] It follows that if a republic wants to secure its freedom, it must attain that greatness which permits it to defend itself without being dependent on somebody else's help. A republic or a principality must pursue territorial greatness to attain security, not through conquest and predation but through appropriate alliances, by protecting and treating with justice subject cities and peoples.

10

REPUBLICAN CONSTITUTION IN A CORRUPT CITY

I believe it is not beyond the purpose of nor does it fail to conform to the discourse written above to consider whether in a corrupt city one can maintain a free state, if there is one, or if it has not been there, whether one can order it. On this thing I say that it is very difficult to do either the one or the other; and although it is almost impossible to give a rule for it, because it would be necessary to proceed according to the degrees of corruption, nonetheless, since it is good to reason about everything, I do not wish to omit this. I shall presuppose a very corrupt city, by which I shall the more increase such a difficulty, for neither laws nor orders can be found that are enough to check a universal corruption. For as good customs have need of laws to maintain themselves, so laws have need of good customs so as to be observed. Besides this, orders and laws made in a republic at its birth, when men were good, are no longer to the purpose later, when they have become wicked. If laws vary according to the accidents in a city, its orders never vary, or rarely; this makes new laws insufficient because the orders, which remain fixed, corrupt them. [. . .]

If Rome wished to maintain itself free in corruption, therefore, it was necessary that it should have made new orders, as in the course of its life it had made new laws. For one should order different orders and modes of life in a bad subject and in a good one; nor can there be a similar form in a matter altogether contrary. But because these orders have to be renewed either all at a stroke, when they are discovered to be no longer good, or little by little, before they are recognized by everyone, I say that both of these things are almost impossible. For if one wishes to renew them little by little, the cause of it must be someone prudent who sees this inconvenience from very far away and when it arises. It is a very easy thing for not one of these [men] ever to emerge in a city and if indeed one does emerge, that he never be able to persuade anyone else of what he himself understands. For men used to living in one mode do not wish to vary it, and so much the more when they do not look the evil in its face but have to have it shown to them by conjecture. As to innovating these orders at a stroke, when everyone knows that they are not good, I say that the uselessness, which is easily recognized, is difficult to correct. For to do this, it is not enough to use ordinary terms, since the ordinary modes are bad; but it is necessary to go to the extraordinary, such as violence and arms, and before everything else become prince of that city, able to dispose it in one's own mode. Because the reordering of a city for a political way of life presupposes a good man, and becoming prince of a republic by violence presupposes a bad man, one will find that it very rarely happens that someone good wishes to become prince by bad ways, even though his end be good, and that someone wicked, having become prince, wishes to work well, and that it will ever occur to his mind to use well the authority that he has acquired badly. From all the things written above arises the difficulty, or the impossibility, of maintaining a republic in corrupt cities or of creating it anew. If indeed one had to create or maintain one there, it would be necessary to turn it more toward a kingly state than toward a popular state, so that the men who cannot be corrected by the laws because of their insolence should be checked in some mode by an almost kingly power.

Discourses on Livy, *I.18*

Machiavelli worried about the political and moral corruption that destroys civil and political life: the corruption of the customs, of the habits of the citizens and their unwillingness to put the common good above private or factional interest. Corruption is also an absence of virtue, a kind of laziness, of ineptitude for political activity, or lack of moral or physical strength to resist tyranny and to stop ambitious men imposing their domination. Whereas in a free republic the law rules over men, in the corrupt republic laws are disobeyed. When the citizens are corrupt, he writes, 'good laws are of no avail' (*D*, I.16) and a 'most corrupt city' is one in which 'there will be found neither laws nor institutions which will suffice to check widespread corruption' (*D*, I.18).

Corruption is a disease that penetrates the deepest fibres of collective life, and perverts a citizen's manners and judgement. Machiavelli's clearest portrait of the corrupt republic is to be found in the *Florentine Histories*, where an anonymous citizen describes the state of the city during the struggle between the Ricci and the Albizzi: 'the young are lazy, the old lascivious; both sexes at every age are full of foul customs, for which good laws, because they are spoiled by wicked use, are no remedy. From this grows the avarice that is seen in our citizens and the appetite, not for true glory, but for the contemptible honours on which hatreds, enmities, differences, and sects depend; and from these arise deaths, exiles, persecution of the good, exaltation of the wicked'. In the corrupt republic there is no true civic friendship. Citizens form groups only to do evil against the fatherland, or against other citizens. There is no mutual trust, as oaths and faiths are respected only as long as they are useful or can be used to deceive. The citizens' judgement on persons and actions, and the citizens' language, are perverted: harmful men are praised as industrious and good men are blamed as fools (*FH*, III.5).

Along with a careful diagnosis of corruption, Machiavelli devotes large sections of the *Discourses* to investigating its causes. He points first to the servile origin of cities. A city which 'at the outset was in servitude to another', he remarks, 'should find it not merely difficult, but impossible, ever to draw up a constitution that will enable it to enjoy tranquillity in the conduct of its affairs' (D, I.49). The example is Florence, which, founded under the emperors and having always lived under foreign rule, remained for a time 'abject' and incapable of taking care of itself. When it attained some liberty, it attempted to establish a good political constitution, but since the new political orders were mingled with the old ones that were unfit for free government, they turned out to be no good. For this reason Florence has never had a political regime that could be properly called a republic.

Another cause of corruption is princely or monarchical rule. Peoples living for a long time under a prince acquire servile habits; they do not know how to govern themselves, how to deliberate on public matters or how to defend their republic from external enemies. If by chance they become free, they soon fall under the domination of another prince (D, I.16). It was therefore a great fortune for Rome that the kings 'quickly became corrupt, with the result that they were expelled before their corruption had penetrated to the bowels of that city' (D, I.17). When the Roman people was not corrupt, it was capable of defending the liberty it had attained after the expulsion of the kings. But when it became 'extremely corrupt', it was unable to preserve the liberty that was regained when Caesar was killed, and even when Gaius Caligula and Nero were killed and 'the whole of Caesar's stock was exterminated' (D, I.17).

Corruption produced by princely government erodes the citizens' moral and physical strength: instead of learning how to serve the common good, they learn to serve powerful men and get used to depending on somebody's will. Personal dependence and therefore corruption are caused by 'absolute power' and exaggerated wealth. Absolute power, says Machiavelli, can very soon corrupt even a virtuous city, because whoever has such a power can have friends and partisans – that is, citizens who are loyal to him, and not to the constitution (*D*, I. 35). Exaggerated wealth is a source of corruption for a similar reason. Wealthy citizens can easily obtain power incompatible with civic equality by doing private favours, such as lending money, paying for dowries and protecting felons from the magistrates. They form powerful cohorts of partisans and friends who feel even more encouraged to become 'corrupters of public morals and law breakers' (*D*, III.28).

Another cause of personal dependence and therefore of corruption is the 'gentry' – people who live 'in idleness on the abundant revenues derived from their estates, without having anything to do either with their cultivation or with other forms of labour essential to life'. They are pernicious to civil life not only because of their idle way of living, but also, and above all, because they have subjects who are 'under their obedience' and therefore dependent on them. For this reason no republic and no political life has lasted for long in the Kingdom of Naples, Rome, Romagna or Lombardy, where the gentry are numerous and powerful. Rightly, therefore, German free cities that want to preserve their 'political and uncorrupted' way of life kill the gentry whenever they have the chance (*D*, I.55).

The redemption of a corrupt republic can be attempted either by the peaceful means of reform, or through violence and absolute authority. Machiavelli strongly urges the former. To use extraordinary means to institute a republic in a corrupt city, one must become prince of the city and dispose of it as one thinks fit. To reorder a city to political life needs a good man; yet only a bad man can gain absolute power. Therefore, Machiavelli concludes, 'very rarely will there be found a good man ready to use bad methods in order to make himself prince, though with a good end in view, nor yet a bad man who, having become a prince, is ready to do the right thing and to whose mind it will occur to use well that authority which he has acquired by bad means' (*D*, I.18). A similar warning is made in the *Florentine Histories*, where a patriot ends his exhortation to the Signoria to restore a 'true free and civil life' to Florence by stressing that it is better 'to do now, with the benignity of the laws, that which, after deferring, men may be required by necessity to do with the support of arms' (*FH*, III.5).

It is very difficult to restore political life in a corrupt city through peaceful reform. Reform could be peacefully carried out if a prudent man sees the weaknesses of existing orders and persuades his fellow citizens to change them. But prudent men rarely arise, and even more rarely do they manage to persuade citizens to change their accustomed mode of life to prevent an evil that they do not yet see. The reform of the city through ordinary means is, like reform through violence and absolute authority, almost impossible. This does not suggest that it should not be attempted. It simply means that only extraordinary men will be able to carry it out. By their outstanding virtue and courage, they will give life to new orders that will restrain men's ambition and insolence. These exceptional citizens must not hesitate to use quasi-regal power when doing so. Machiavelli encourages a shift towards monarchical government because, of the three elements that ought to form a well-ordered government – namely the monarchical, the aristocratic and the popular – one, the monarchical (or executive) element, has to have for a while predominance over the other (*D*, I.18).

That the restoration of political life can only be accomplished by a man who uses quasi-regal authority does not contradict Machiavelli's commitment to the principles of civil life nor his belief that the best form of government is a mixed government that includes a quasi-monarchical element, such as lifetime magistrates like the gonfaloniere in Florence (between 1503 and 1512) or the doge in Venice. Nor is Machiavelli's emphasis on the extraordinary virtue of founders and redeemers incompatible with his advocacy of the rule of law, which is at the core of his republicanism. In the formative moments of the republic, when laws are not in place, and in moments of crisis, when the laws are not respected because of omnipresent corruption, it is necessary for a founder or redeemer to use his outstanding virtue to institute the laws or to restore the strength of legality. The restoration of liberty in a corrupt city is due, as Machiavelli remarks, to the 'simple virtue of one man alone independently of any law' (*D*, III.1). It is a 'simple virtue' which does not supplant the rule of law, but establishes or restores it. Rule of law and rule of men are both essential components of Machiavelli's republican theory. One cannot exist, or continue to exist, without the other. When the rule of law has not yet been instituted, or when it has been spoiled by corruption, it is time for men's virtue to bring about the rule of law or give laws and statutes a new life (*D*, III.30). Once the foundational or redemptive work is completed, the care of the republic must be entrusted to the citizens, and they must hold it dear, and serve it with their utmost devotion and wisdom, if it is to last.

NOTES

1 Ernst Cassirer, *The Myth of the State* (New Haven, Yale University Press, 1946), p. 130.
2 *Opere*, vol. II, p. 774–5.
3 B. Latini, *Li livres dou tresor*, in F. J. Carmody (ed.) (Berkeley and Los Angeles, University of California Press, 1948), Book I, Chapter 4.
4 C. Salutati, *De nobilitate legum et medicinae*, in E. Garin (ed.) (Florence, 1947), p. 168.
5 *Ibid.*, p. 170.
6 *Ibid.*, p. 170.
7 Leonardo Bruni Aretino, *Humanistische-Philosophische Schriften* (Leipzig and Berlin, 1928), p. 73.
8 See F. Gilbert, 'Florentine Political Assumptions', in *Journal of the Warburg and Courtauld Institutes*, 20 (1957), p. 208.
9 See F. Gilbert, 'Florentine Political Assumptions', in *Journal of the Warburg and Courtauld Institutes*, 20 (1957), p. 208.
10 Francesco Guicciardini, *Dialogue on the Government of Florence*, Alison Brown (ed.) (Cambridge University Press, 1994), p. 159.
11 Angelo Poliziano, 'Oratio Super Fabio Quintiliano et Statii Sylvis', in Eugenio Garin (ed.), *Prosatori Latini del Quattrocento* (Milano–Napoli, Ricciardi, date unknown), pp. 883–5.
12 *The Miscellaneous Works of Lord Macaulay* (New York and London, Harper & Bros, 1899), vol. I, pp. 69–71 and 122.
13 Carlo Curcio, *Machiavelli nel Risorgimento* (Milano, Giuffré, 1953) pp. 22–3.
14 Cicero, *Of the Orator*, II.IX.36.
15 *Institutio Oratoria*, III.VIII, pp. 66–7.
16 *Institutio Oratoria*, XIII.II, pp. 29–31.
17 Leonardo Aretino, *Istoria Fiorentina*, tradotta in volgare da Donato Acciajuoli (Florence, Le Monnier, 1861) pp. 3–4.
18 *Ibid.*, p. 4.
19 *Istoria di M. Poggio Fiorentino*, tradotta di Latino in Volgare da Iacopo suo figliuolo (Florence, Filippo Giunti, 1598) pp. 1–2.
20 Felix Gilbert, 'Machiavelli: The Renaissance of the Art of War', in

P. Paret (ed.), *Makers of Modern Strategy* (Princeton University Press, 1986), p. 24.

21 'Discursus Florentinarum Rerum', in *Opere*, vol. I, p. 744.

22 On the distinction between fame and glory in Roman republican political theory, see Donald Earl, *The Moral and Political Tradition of Rome* (Ithaca, New York, Cornell University Press, 1967), p. 30.

23 'Discursus florentinarum rerum', in *Opere*, vol. I, p. 739.

24 'Parole da dirle sopra la provisione del danaio, facto un poco di proemio et di scusa', in *Opere*, vol. I, pp. 12–15.

CHRONOLOGY

1469 Niccolò di Bernardo Machiavelli is born in Florence on 3 May. His mother is Bartolomea de' Nelli.

1476 Niccolò attends grammar school.

1481 He studies Latin under the guidance of Paolo da Ronciglione.

1486 Bernardo Machiavelli brings home a copy of Livy's *History of Rome*, on which Niccolò will base his *Discourses on Livy*.

1498 Machiavelli is appointed Head of the Second Chancery of the Republic of Florence; he then also becomes Secretary to the Ten of Liberty and Peace. His main duty is to assist the Signoria in matters of international affairs and the dominion. He is very close to Gonfaloniere Pier Soderini, the highest officer of the Florentine Republic.

1499 Mission to Forlì, where he meets the Duchess Caterina Sforza.

1500 Niccolò's father Bernardo passes away on 19 May; he completes his first diplomatic mission to France, where he meets King Louis XII and George d'Amboise, Cardinal of Rouen.

1501 He marries Marietta di Luigi Corsini, who will give him seven sons: Primerana, Bernardo, Lodovico, Piero, Guido, Bartolomea (or Baccia or Baccina) and Totto.

1502–3 He helps to make the office of Gonfaloniere a lifetime appointment. (The Gonfaloniere was the highest magistrate of the Republic with powers of representation and coordination of the various institutes of the Florentine government.) He composes an oration for the collection of money to provide Florence with an adequate military defence (*Words to Speak on Providing Money*). Diplomatic missions to Caesar Borgia, the very ambitious and able son of Pope Alexander VI, who wanted to establish a principality in central Italy and then fell from power after the death of his father.

1504 Second mission to France to meet with King Louis XII. He composes the *First Decennial*, a history in verse of Florence and Italy from 1494. Diplomatic missions to Mantua and Siena.

1506 He is sent on a diplomatic mission to Pope Julius II.

1506 He organizes the first instalment of a Florentine militia, composed of soldiers from the contado, and writes the poem *Of Fortune*.

1507–8 He undertakes a mission to the Emperor Maximilian.

1509 Florentine troops attack Pisa; Machiavelli heads the negotiations that lead to the city's surrender.

1510–11 Two missions to the court of France to discuss the issue of the schismatic Gallican Council, held first in Pisa and then in Milan.

1512 After the Sack of Prato by Spanish and papal armies, Soderini's republic is overthrown and the Medici return to power in Florence.

1513 Machiavelli is dismissed from his office, tried, sentenced to one year's confinement within the Florentine dominion, then imprisoned and tortured under the charge of conspiracy against the newly restored Medicean government. He is freed in March, after Giovanni de' Medici is elected pope under the name of Leo X. He retires to his family properties in the countryside, in Sant'Andrea in Percussina, where he works on the *Discourses on Livy* and completes *De Principatibus*, a short work destined to become famous as *The Prince*.

1515–16 He writes *The [Golden] Ass*, an unfinished poem, and frequents the Orti Oricellari, a gathering of the young Florentine aristocracy, where he discusses his ideas on the imitation of Roman republican politics.

1518 He composes a comedy, *Mandragola,* an instant success and one of the greatest works of Italian theatre, and the fable *Belfagor, or The Devil Who Took A Wife*.

1519 Publication of *Mandragola*.

1520 Having composed *The Life of Castruccio Castracani*, a captain of Lucca (1281–1328), he receives from Cardinal Giulio de' Medici (later Pope Clement VII) the commission to write a history of Florence. He also composes, again by invitation of Cardinal Giulio de' Medici, a proposal for a new constitution to ensure Florence a peaceful transition from the Medicis' regime to a republican government (*Discourse on Florentine Public Affairs after the Death of the Junior Lorenzo*).

1521 The government of Florence sends Machiavelli to Carpi to settle matters concerning the jurisdiction over the monasteries of the Minor Friars. There he befriends Francesco Guicciardini. He publishes *The Art of War*, a dialogue in which he encourages a return to ancient Roman military orders and spirit. It is his only political or historical work to appear in print during his lifetime, although all his writings were circulated in manuscript copies.

1525 He composes another comedy, *Clizia*, and a *Discourse or Dialogue on our Language*. His authorship of this work has been long disputed.

1526 He presents the *Florentine Histories* to Pope Clement VII.

1527 He composes a sermon to a lay religious confraternity (*Exhortation to Penitence*). Spanish and German soldiers sack Rome. In Florence, the Medici are overthrown and the republican government restored. Machiavelli dies on 21 June and is buried in Santa Croce.

1531 Posthumous publication of *Discourses on Livy*, which required the permission of the papal court.

1532 Posthumous publication of *The Prince*, again with the permission of the papal court.

1559 Machiavelli's works are placed on the Index of Prohibited Books instituted by the papal court. They can no longer be sold, read or quoted. His name cannot be cited in books.

1640 First English translation of *The Prince*, by Edward Dacres.

SUGGESTIONS FOR FURTHER READING

Works by Machiavelli in English

The Prince, trans. Peter Bondanella, introduction by Maurizio Viroli (Oxford University Press, 2005).

Discourses on Livy, ed. and trans. Harvey C. Mansfield and Nathan Tarcov (University of Chicago Press, 1996).

Florentine Histories, ed. and trans. Laura F. Banfield and Harvey C. Mansfield, Jr (Princeton University Press, 1988).

The Art of War, ed. and trans. Christopher Lynch (University of Chicago Press, 2003).

Machiavelli and His Friends: Their Personal Correspondence, ed. and trans. James B. Atkinson and David Sices (Dekalb, Northern Illinois University Press, 1996).

The Mandrake Root in *The Portable Machiavelli*, ed. and trans. Peter Bondanella and Mark Musa (New York, Penguin, 1979).

Readers

Machiavelli: The Chief Works and Others, ed. and trans. Allan Gilbert (Durham, NC: Duke University Press, 1965), 3 vols.

Machiavelli's life

Roberto Ridolfi, *The Life of Niccolò Machiavelli* (University of Chicago Press, 1963).

Sebastian de Grazia, *Machiavelli in Hell* (Princeton University Press, 1989).

Maurizio Viroli, *Niccolò's Smile: A Biography of Machiavelli*, trans. Anthony Shugaar (New York, Farrar, Straus and Giroux, 2002).

Historical and intellectual context

Quentin Skinner, *The Foundations of Modern Political Thought* (Cambridge University Press, 1978), 2 vols.

John A. G. Pocock, *The Machiavellian Moment: Florentine Political Thought and the Atlantic Republican Tradition* (Princeton University Press, 1975).

Maurizio Viroli, *From Politics to Reason of State* (Cambridge University Press, 1992).

Gisela Bock, Quentin Skinner and Maurizio Viroli (eds.), *Machiavelli and Republicanism* (Cambridge University Press, 1990).

Felix Gilbert, *Machiavelli and Guicciardini: Politics and History in Sixteenth-Century Florence* (Princeton University Press, 1965).

J. R. Hale, *Machiavelli and Renaissance Italy* (London, English University Press, 1961).

Hans Baron, *The Crisis of the Early Italian Renaissance* (Princeton University Press, 1966).

Studies on Machiavelli's political and philosophical ideas

Isaiah Berlin, 'The Originality of Machiavelli', in *Against the Current* (New York, Viking Press, 1980) pp. 25–79.

Hans Baron, 'Machiavelli: The Republican Citizen and the Author of *The Prince*', in *English Historical Review*, 76 (1961), pp. 217–53.

Marcia Colish, 'The Idea of Liberty in Machiavelli', in *Journal of the History of Ideas*, 32 (1971), pp. 323–51.

Eugene Garver, *Machiavelli and the History of Prudence* (Madison, University of Wisconsin Press, 1987).

A. H. Gilbert, *Machiavelli's Prince and its Forerunners: The 'Prince' as a Typical Book de Regimine Principum* (Durham, NC, Duke University Press, 1938).

Mark Hulliung, *Citizen Machiavelli* (Princeton University Press, 1983).

Victoria Kahn, *Machiavellian Rhetoric: From the Counter-Reformation to Milton* (Princeton University Press, 1994).

Harvey C. Mansfield, *Machiavelli's Virtue* (University of Chicago Press, 1996).

Anthony Parel, *The Machiavellian Cosmos* (New Haven, Yale University Press, 1992).

Anthony Parel, *The Political Calculus: Essays on Machiavelli's Philosophy* (University of Toronto Press, 1972).

Hanna Pitkin, *Fortune is a Woman: Gender and Politics in the Thought of Niccolò Machiavelli* (Berkeley and Los Angeles, University of California Press, 1975).

Quentin Skinner, *Machiavelli* (New York, Hill and Wang, 1981).

Vickie B. Sullivan, *Machiavelli's Three Romes: Religion, Human Liberty, and Politics Reformed* (Dekalb, Northern Illinois University Press, 1996).

Maurizio Viroli, *Machiavelli* (Oxford University Press, 1998).

INDEX